31969027107803

MY LIFE
— ON THE —
LINE

HOW THE NFL DAMN NEAR KILLED ME, AND ENDED UP SAVING MY LIFE

D0002094

RYAN O'CALLAGHAN
WITH CYD ZEIGLER

EDGE
OF SPORTS

My Life on the Line is the latest title in Dave Zirin's **Edge of Sports** imprint. Addressing issues across many different sports at both the professional and nonprofessional/collegiate level, Edge of Sports aims to provide an even deeper articulation of the daily collision between sports and politics, giving cutting-edge writers the opportunity to fully explore their areas of expertise in book form.

All rights reserved. No part of this book may be reproduced, stored in a retrieval system, or transmitted in any form, by any means, including mechanical, electronic, photocopying, recording, or otherwise, without the prior written consent of the publisher.

Published by Akashic Books
©2019 Ryan O'Callaghan and Cyd Zeigler

Paperback ISBN: 978-1-61775-759-4
Hardcover ISBN: 978-1-61775-758-7
Library of Congress Control Number: 2019935372
All rights reserved

Edge of Sports
c/o Akashic Books
Brooklyn, New York, USA
Ballydehob, Co. Cork, Ireland
Twitter: @AkashicBooks
Facebook: AkashicBooks
E-mail: info@akashicbooks.com
Website: www.akashicbooks.com

ALSO FROM EDGE OF SPORTS

You Throw Like a Girl: The Blind Spot of Masculinity
by Don McPherson

*Fair Play: How LGBT Athletes Are
Claiming Their Rightful Place in Sports*
by Cyd Zeigler

Tigerbelle: The Wyomia Tyus Story
by Wyomia Tyus & Elizabeth Terzakis

We Matter: Athletes and Activism
by Etan Thomas

*Unsportsmanlike Conduct:
College Football and the Politics of Rape*
by Jessica Luther

Chasing Water: Elegy of an Olympian
by Anthony Ervin & Constantine Markides

This book is dedicated to all of my friends and family who have supported me over the years and helped me put my life back together. I now see that your love was always there.

I've written this book for all of the people who find themselves in dark places. When the people around you tell you they love you, they mean it. I hope my story brings that truth to light for you.

—Ryan

Table of Contents

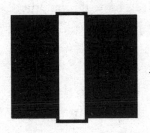

Introduction: Crypt Keeper

We've been planting trees all afternoon, and I'm beat. It's an unseasonably warm day in May, so I'm sweating even worse than usual. Dustin brought a bunch of willow trees to plant around the lake at my cabin. He's a freaking plant whisperer. The guy loves nature and hard work as much as I do. There we are in the middle of the off-season doing hard, manual labor. It feels good.

I have the muscle, so I do the digging. Dustin Colquitt is our team's punter for the Kansas City Chiefs, so he points out spots around the lake that he thinks will be good places for the trees. And yeah, he does some of the digging too. Shovel in hand, plant, scoop, throw. Plant, scoop, throw. Plant, scoop, throw. It's a lot easier than blocking 280-pound defensive ends. After the season I had, it's a lot more enjoyable too. An injury and an idiot coach put me on the bench for most of the previous year. Now we're on strike and the league has locked the players out over some bullshit, so we're not able to go to the team facility. The only thing that wasn't a mess for me with the team that season was my paycheck. I had finally had a big payday. That made it possible to buy the property and build this cabin. I need the place to escape more than anyone else knows.

"Okay, bring it over," I wave to Dustin and my best friend Brian. Brian and I had been two musketeers in high school. Our teenage pact was that if one of us made it in football, the other would come along for the ride. It was a good deal for him in high school since he wasn't exactly going to the NFL anytime soon. We had drifted apart while I was in college, but my word is my word. Plus, Brian is a resourceful guy to have around. When I landed my first NFL contract, I had officially made it. And so Brian came along for the ride.

It's the last tree, and Dustin wants to "do the honors." He lifts the five-foot willow and drops it into the hole. He and I push the dirt over the root ball, Brian soaks it with the hose, and we all back away.

On paper, Dustin is exactly the kind of guy I try to avoid: a superreligious Bible thumper. It's no secret what guys like Dustin think of a fag like me. If only he knew. But something about Dustin disarms me a bit. Sure, he is praying and preaching all the time, but he has this way of making me feel like I matter as a person. I never go near the church stuff with him, and maybe he sees a non-Christian like me as a challenge, a guy he has to help "save" to get on God's good side. Whatever it is in his head, I always have a good time with him despite all the God stuff. Still, he is just about the last person on earth I'll ever tell my secret.

When Dustin isn't leading Bible study in the locker room, we're talking about how to improve the land on my property. It seems every day in the Chiefs locker room we are talking about nature. He is out at the property whenever he can be. Between football and his family, he doesn't have much free time, but like me, he gravitates toward the land. The land is his escape too. A couple weeks earlier when I mentioned planting some trees, he knew exactly what to get. These gorgeous willows. He is an artist with this kind of stuff.

"This is what I miss," Dustin says, beaming at our achievement, looking over the lake and the trees he'd brought, now standing on the shore of the lake. "In ten years these willows are gonna be the most beautiful things on this property," he adds, throwing back a swig of beer.

"Second," Brian snorts, a chuckle bubbling out. "In ten years I hope his wife is more beautiful than those trees."

That gets a laugh from Dustin.

Should I respond? Add to it? Just agree? If I say the wrong thing it could blow my cover. Or raise eyebrows. What would a straight guy say here? What would Dustin say? He's superreligious. And I'm a football player. They're not even thinking about me being gay. At least, Dustin isn't. Is Brian? I'm not sweating about Brian. What should I say that doesn't sound like I'm trying to figure out what Dustin would say? I got it.

"Amen." I glance at Dustin. *Was that it? Did I get it right? Shit, did I blow it? Too cute?*

"Aaaaaaaaa-MEN!" Dustin takes another swig, still admiring his contribution to the property.

Phew.

Brian jumps in: "If we're gonna get the fish today, we gotta go before they close."

Dustin's second brainstorm is to get a bunch of algae-eating fish for the three-acre pond on the property. The lake is so full of algae that from the satellite view you can't even tell there is water. Dustin said these fish—koi or some shit like that—would take care of the problem. I swear, when he's done in the league he'll run a landscaping company.

"You guys go ahead," I say. "I'm gonna work inside."

In a flash they are in a white GMC Sierra 2500 Denali headed for town. While the truck is registered in my name, I let Brian use it like it's his. He is the only one who ever drives it, so I think everyone assumes it is his. I've always had big trucks.

At my size, they just work a lot better than a BMW or Jaguar or some of the other cars the littler guys on the team drive. Plus, the big truck says "straight." That is as important to me as the fit of the cab.

As they head off down the driveway, my shoulders relax, my smile fades. While I genuinely enjoy spending time with both of them, it is also exhausting. Being with anyone is exhausting. I have to be "on" all the time, constantly building the character I am playing in my own life, burying my deep, dark secret for the fun-loving, rich NFL player living out all of the fantasies of his fake adult life. It is when I am alone that I can ditch the act, left with the depression that grows every day I get closer to the end of my career.

The sun is just setting, so I go inside to tackle the next project. The dogs, Rodger and Taylor, nip at my heels, already looking for an early dinner, as I walk up the steps of the front porch.

In a rural area of Independence, Missouri, the cabin is as rustic-looking as I can get it without it looking like a shack. Double glass doors open up to a small first floor with an outhouse–sized bathroom complete with a fake indoor tin roof and cedar-shake siding. The vaulted ceiling makes it feel a lot bigger than it is. Up the spiral staircase is the loft-style bedroom that extends out over part of the porch. I modeled it after the hunting lodges I'd seen in Northern California all my childhood.

I walk in the doors and click on the stereo. Jason Aldean, one of my new favorites, pipes through the speakers. What I love about country music is the melancholy attitude so much of it has when it's done right. Not that poppy shit you sometimes hear today. I'm talking real, solid country music. Jason Aldean hits it with every song. There's a loneliness about his music that speaks to me. Loneliness always has.

Plus, I love the stories country music tells. Sure, those stories are about beer, trucks, dogs, guns, tractors, and girls. But I drink a lot of beer. I own two trucks and two dogs. I have a bunch of guns. Hell, I even own a tractor I've spent hours riding, moving around dirt and building roads that crisscross my property. The only thing I don't have is a girl. All the swooning and singing about girls just makes listening to country music that much better for my image. Gay guys listen to Madonna. I listen to Garth Brooks.

I drink beer in part because that says "straight" too. I already downed a six-pack this afternoon, so I dive into the small fridge for more. I crack open a can of Busch Light and guzzle it in a couple swigs. Our backup quarterback, Brodie Croyle, has gotten me drinking that stuff when we go down to his cabin on off days. I open another one and start in on that.

Finally I come to the real reason I sent the guys on their way. I open a drawer and pull out my bottle of eighty-milligram OxyContin. I used to keep weed out here, but the league put a stop to that. Instead I'm now downing enough painkillers every day to kill the average person. At six foot six and 330 pounds I'm twice the average person. I don't want Brian or anyone else to know just how many painkillers I'm doing, so the guys heading to the store is the perfect opportunity. I crush the pill on the counter and snort it.

Aaaaaahhhhh. Peace.

I relish being alone out here. It's just me, the dogs, some beer, the painkillers, and whatever project is next. I always need a project. When I bought the property, it was forty acres of impenetrable wilderness. The property had been used as a Christmas tree farm, so there are gorgeous pines all over, along with pockmarks dotting the land where stumps were pulled. I've built roads, cleared the lakeshore of trees, planted deer plots, erected a fence and a bunch of other shit. When Dustin or a neighbor isn't free to help, it is perfectly isolating.

Keep busy, keep moving. What's next?

I've just installed the gun cabinet and I brought some guns here from my house in town. I've been collecting them for a while and by now I have amassed a huge stockpile of weapons. Collecting guns is a hobby of Brian's that I've gotten a bit hooked on. I stacked the ones I brought in the corner this morning so I can shine them up before putting them in the case. I have enough for me and a dozen friends to trudge into the snow chasing the deer. I grab a rag and some gun polish and sit on the couch next to the guns. One by one I rub them to a shine. Always have to make sure the guns look good. They are part of the show.

Truth is, I hate deer hunting. The idea of sitting in a tree and waiting for a deer to come eat at a food plot I've set up is literally one of the stupidest things I've ever heard in my life. My buddies don't think so. Killing things is part of being a man. One time Brian shot a deer out here. Bad shot, hit it in the shoulder but didn't kill it. We had to track that thing and put a few more bullets in it before it would go down. Chasing that wounded deer, as it felt the entire world closing in on it, knowing we were out to get it—that fucking broke my heart. I'll never let Brian or the other guys know, but I felt that deer's pain. It brought me back to the first time I shot a deer, when I was a kid.

It was cold, hunting season. When I pulled the trigger and that deer went down with an audible thud, my dad was as happy as I'd seen him. Killing deer was a rite of passage for the O'Callaghans. I was suddenly a man. But when I walked up to that deer's dead body, I swear it was staring at me, right into my soul, this innocent animal that had just been wandering around looking for something to eat. I was out there killing deer so nobody would think I was gay, taking something's life just for show.

So fucked up.

When I finish polishing the guns, I set each one carefully in the gun cabinet.

The time is coming when I will finally use one of those guns on my property. My injuries are mounting. Chiefs coach Todd Haley already has a role in taking away my starting position, a mixture of superstition and his tiff with our general manager, Scott Pioli, who brought me over from the New England Patriots. I figure I have at least a few years left in the NFL, though. With the dirt I have on one of my coaches, maybe a little more.

Once my NFL career is over I'll get in the truck, drive to the property, open this gun cabinet, and shoot myself in the head.

I'm not building a cabin. I'm building a crypt.

Nobody wants a fucking faggot around.

Chapter 1: Different

I'm in the NFL, playing for the Kansas City Chiefs. I have a beautiful property with a cabin I love. A kick-ass truck. Two great dogs. My neighborhood takes pride in me simply living there. When I talk, people listen. And when I wear that Chiefs jersey, everybody wants to be around me. I have the money to do just about anything I want, whenever I want. Most guys in America would kill to have the life I have. I'm on top of the world.

Yet I'm still that little gay kid who grew up in the middle of nowhere, scared quite literally to death. The secret that I buried inside of me at a very young age is something disgusting, unacceptable, deadly. No matter who I am or what I accomplish, the revelation of that secret will destroy my life and push away anyone who learns it. Being gay is death.

In the early nineties, before I was even a teenager, gays were the butts of jokes on TV, in movies, and in any conversation around the house that needed a punch line. I did not hear a positive word said about a gay person throughout my entire childhood. Even unknowingly, the way my mother talked about the gay doctor she worked for hit at my core. She never said anything hateful about him. Heck, he was her boss and she knew he was gay. But she would talk about him dying soon in a matter-of-fact way, like all gay men die young. She'd share secondhand stories of his gay parties with his friends in a way that told me they were, like every other gay man, quite simply signing their own death warrants with a stream of endless drugs and sex. My mom's comments were the nicest I ever heard about gay people, even though they were just matter-of-fact about death and drugs. For everyone else, gay guys were the "fags with AIDS" down in San Francisco who seemingly everybody in my formative years just wished would go away. I heard something like that message all the time.

I grew up in a man's-man family. The O'Callaghans were spread all across Northern California from the biggest cities to the smallest towns. My dad, his cousins, and their wives and kids were all traditional American families. "Red-blooded Americans." The men worked in mills and firehouses, the women made dinner and took care of the kids and maybe had a small side job. There was a mold for what each of us was supposed to look and act like, and there was simply no breaking the mold in my family.

I saw my extended family a lot, and every gathering reinforced what kind of O'Callaghan I was supposed to be. Our family barbecues were often at Hendy Woods, a state park two hundred miles south full of redwood groves. It was like venturing onto Endor. I hated it. Not because of the place, which was very cool. Even back then I loved nature. But those family barbecues, reuniting with O'Callaghans, as well as with my mom's side of the family, were boring as fuck. They reminded me every time what an outsider I was in my own life.

For starters, I had no cousins who were my age. They were all teens or infants. The park was a potential playground with giant, hollow redwood stumps large enough to sneak into. But no one wanted to play hide-and-seek. No one wanted to climb rocks or splash in ponds. Instead, everyone always broke right into their typical gender roles. Without fail, the women would prepare all the food while the men shared their stories, trying desperately to impress one another over cans of beer. They never talked about run-of-the-mill topics like politics or movies. Sometimes sports would enter the conversation, but generally it was an afternoon of one-upmanship, where each of them would take turns trying to impress the other guys with a story about a new toy or property he bought or how manly he was.

I always thought my dad was quietly envious of the money my uncles had. They would casually drop hints about things they bought or trips they'd go on with their families. There was a simple ease about their lives, being able to buy whatever they wanted, that my dad seemed to yearn for. It was a lot harder for my dad to build wealth. Among his cousins, he was the only one who didn't grow up around money. His parents were dirt poor. I mean *dirt* poor. He started helping to support his parents when he was twelve. He simply started from a much tougher spot.

As I approached my teenage years, my place at these reunions was set. Despite feeling more comfortable slicing tomatoes with the women, I had to stand around with the beer drinkers. The "fags with AIDS" were, for whatever reason, also a popular topic.

"So these two gay guys meet on the street," my uncle John started the conversation with a joke like he always did. He was a firefighter in San Francisco all through the AIDS crisis. He had story upon story about helping gay guys, none of them positive.

Here we go again.

"One of them is blind, and they go back to the blind man's apartment," he continued, grinning ear to ear, anticipating the punch line that would again prove his manhood. "The blind man asks the other guy if he wants to play a game. The game is to shove stuff up the blind man's ass, and he'll tell the other guy what it is."

It almost always had to do with putting something up some guy's ass.

"The guy grabs a kielbasa, shoves it up the blind man's ass, and of course he knew what it was. Then the guy grabs a rolling pin. Same result. So then he goes to the bathroom and grabs a . . ." Uncle John held his beer bottle with both hands moving it up and down, to simulate using a plunger in a toilet.

"A plunger," my dad said.

"Oh, you've played the game before!"

Laughter ensued. Looking back, the joke is kind of funny. But for them, anything that made fun of those fags with AIDS in San Francisco was a testament to manhood that resonated with every single man in my family.

Yet every joke that made fun of them . . . made fun of me. I had to stand there among the men and take it. I had to like it. I had to laugh. I watched my dad joke right along with them, then weigh in himself.

"How do you fit three queers on one barstool?" my dad asked, the guys leaning in, playing the role.

Shrugs and grins, all waiting for the laugh.

"Turn it upside down!"

Even as a young kid I knew the jokes were about me. But it wasn't just the jokes. The men in my family showed what seemed like a deep-rooted contempt for gay men. Being a kid who knew he was a bit different, hearing the people I loved talk about the "fags," and it often had to do with those fags having some deadly disease—it really sucked, because it made me think that in their eyes I was just a fag too. That got to me a lot. I didn't call myself "gay" at the time. Kissing anyone wasn't on my radar screen, and I didn't even know what sex was. But I knew I liked being near other boys in a way that I felt I had to keep to myself, in a way that I could never tell another living soul, especially the men in my family.

The time I had a real inkling that I was different from the other boys was during a family trip to Lake Tahoe. We went every year with aunts, uncles, and cousins. One day on this particular trip when I was about seven, my uncle Greg thought it would be a hoot to write *Hooter Patrol* on the T-shirts of my cousin and me. My cousin Derek loved it. A year older than I, he thought it was the best idea in the world that we would now be walking up to women and looking at their boobs. I had absolutely no interest in any of it, even though I watched my cousin and uncle seem to be loving the idea. It was a struggle for me to even pretend to be interested. That day in Tahoe trying to look at anything but boobs, I knew beyond any doubt that I was different, and that I was going to have to put on an act so that nobody would ever know just how different I was.

Another good hint was my interest in *Saved by the Bell*. Instead of the cute girls on the show, I knew it was because of Zack Morris that I watched every week. I guess everyone who was a gay kid in the early nineties has the same story about that dorky show. But I sure didn't think it was dorky at the time.

I knew beyond any doubt that I was gay when I was about thirteen and hit puberty. Suddenly my interest in being near boys became an interest in being naked near them, in kissing them. I would catch myself looking at other boys, my stare lingering just a second too long. I would consciously tell myself I had to stop doing it or I would lose all of my friends. At the time, my friends were the kids in the band. I had no self-esteem, and I was shy about approaching any of the popular kids, in part because they were often the most attractive guys in the school, and that intimidated me. I didn't want anyone thinking I was trying to hang out with the hot guys, because that's what fags did. So I stuck with my friends in the band, even though I'd given up the clarinet in third grade.

There was one moment I remember that made me feel better about myself, hiding quietly in my little corner of the world. When Ellen DeGeneres came out, I was fourteen years old and truly understood that I was different from all the rest of the boys. Ellen was the complete opposite from me, some celebrity woman in Hollywood. Yet her coming out in the middle of that world did give me some comfort that I wasn't alone. I would still leave the room any time a show like *Will & Grace* came on. I wanted nothing to do with anything that even hinted at the possibility of people being gay. Though I would have never admitted it to anyone around me at the time, Ellen's coming out helped me when I was just figuring out who I was.

Despite all that, by the time I hit Enterprise High School, I was looking for anywhere to hide that I was gay from my family and friends. My hometown is redneck central. Hell, it's called *Red*ding! Everybody thinks about California as this incredibly progressive state where liberalism and acceptance reign from the Pacific to the Sierra Nevadas. Truth is, California is two states: California and Alabama. I lived in Alabama. To give you an idea of the place, Donald Trump beat Hillary Clinton in my county in the 2016 presidential election by thirty-seven points. He beat her in Alabama by less than twenty-eight points.

Redding is also a very Christian place, with a couple of churches within walking distance of my parents' house. It's the home of the Bethel megachurch, which has become one of the most powerful institutions in the city. Every Sunday they draw thousands of people. They even have their own music label now. It's become a cult in Redding. There is a divide in town between those who attend and those who steer clear because they know the crazy ideas being spoon-fed to members at their School of Supernatural Ministry. When the city needed money to pay some cops in 2017, the church donated half a million dollars out of the kindness of their hearts. Of course, a few months later the city okayed the building of a massive new campus for the church. Go figure. Like so many other churches, they use their power and influence to tell people that gay relationships are wrong, and they oppose gay rights by supporting conversion therapy.

While I grew up only a three-hour drive from San Francisco, it felt like seven light-years from the Castro.

Until freshman year I had no problem hanging out with the drama kids and band geeks. But as I got into high school I realized that was the worst hiding spot for a gay kid whose every thought, every move, was becoming consumed by the need to look and act as straight as possible. Entering high school, the group I was hanging out with were the kids getting teased about being weak or gay. It never occurred to me before high school that kids who gravitated toward singing and acting in plays might be seen as gayer than the other kids. They were just fun to hang out with. Suddenly, it was my group of friends who were the butts of gay jokes from the upperclassmen and, increasingly, our own classmates. By then I was already bigger than everybody else in my class, so nobody was going to call me weak. But the gay thing would be, in my head, guilt by association. I couldn't be associated with those kids anymore. I had to make a switch.

I had been in and around the football world since I was a kid. My dad was a high school referee, and he was working his way into the community college ranks. By the time I was in high school, he had made it all the way to the Division I Western Athletic Conference. When I was nine or ten, he started bringing me to some of the Friday-night games. Sometimes I'd be on the sideline, and other times he'd have me shagging balls and helping around the field. As I grew taller and bigger, I heard over and over that I'd have to venture onto the football team once I was old enough.

I never had much of an interest in football. Before high school, I never played the sport. Heck, other than one year of Little League, I never played sports. Running around a court or a field and tossing around some ball full of air just never held my interest. The idea that you have to love football to succeed in it is a bunch of bullshit. It's a myth that guys in and around the sport love to promote, that somehow to get to the pros you have to have some deep-rooted passion for the game itself. Sure, it helps to be pursuing your passion when you're away from your family and friends, getting your ass kicked on a daily basis, but I found another passion in football: hiding.

As the drama kids in my friendship circle were getting teased for allegedly being "gay," the football players never had to deal with that shit. In fact, they were sometimes the ones dealing it out. If you were associated with the football team, you were straight. Period. No questions asked. Ever. So I decided I was going to play football. My dad couldn't have been happier about it. Finally his son was going to take up the mantle of the O'Callaghan men and venture into the macho sports world.

I damn near quit before my football career kicked off. The freshman playbooks weren't the most complicated documents in the world, but there was still a learning curve. Other kids had played football in peewee leagues or other levels for a while. Or they loved football, had been watching it every Saturday and Sunday with their dads for years. I had been to a lot of high school football games, but I was rarely paying very close attention to what was going on on the field. I had a lot of catching up to do.

At my first practice in August, I was hot and sucking wind. The coaches had to spend extra time with me just to show me how to get into a two-point stance. It looks simple enough, just standing there, knees bent, arms ready to block. Yet, like everything, doing it right takes practice. And that first practice I was just fucking it up.

"Goddamnit, O'Callaghan!" one of the coaches screamed. "Watch what I'm fucking doing!"

He got into a stance. It looked just like what I was doing, but his ass was getting lower, getting more leverage. When I tried it again, it was no better and that just elicited more screaming. I'd never been yelled at by an adult other than my parents. I was the good kid, the kid who didn't screw up. To these coaches I was just another dumb freshman who couldn't listen, and they vented all their frustration on me. Getting yelled at nearly pushed me out of football on day one. But I stuck with it and made it through the season, learning to deal with adults who love to yell. It's amazing how many of them find their way into coaching.

By sophomore year the JV coaches were utilizing me on both sides of the ball, and I was overpowering people. That's when other guys on the football team started asking me to hang out with them. If you were helping the football team win games, you were in the popular clique if you wanted to be. I had to be. It sucked to leave my friendship circle I'd spent so many Saturday afternoons with, but by my sophomore year I was desperate to keep any thoughts of me being gay out of people's heads. I knew I didn't want to have to date any girls to prove myself, so I figured that hanging out with the popular guys and kicking ass on the football team would go a long way to keeping my cover.

I also became an asshole. It's one of my biggest regrets from my youth. In my insane quest to prove to the world I was straight, I started harassing the very drama and band kids I had called friends all those years. Except that wasn't me. I had always been one of the good kids. I'm sure a lot of my friends thought the sudden mean streak came from my football success, but the root of it all was really my desperate insecurity about being gay. For my purposes, it all worked. I never heard a peep about me being gay or not dating girls. I showed girls enough fake interest to make it seem like I was just another straight football player.

I have to say, it was a lot of fun being in the popular crowd. When I was with the kids from band and drama, frankly, we didn't do a whole heck of a lot. Being a part of the athlete crowd meant typical teenage house parties, complete with beer that I found I generally liked the taste of. I also really liked the feeling of it. Even then, my size got in the way of getting very drunk. The bigger you are, the more you need to drink to get there. I didn't mind. I was way too afraid that if I did get drunk, I would somehow let something slip about being gay. But I dabbled with alcohol through much of the second half of high school. I was having a lot more fun than I had hanging out with the band kids.

Being in the popular crowd also gave me the deepest friendship of my life. It was early in my junior year that Brian asked me if I wanted to go to lunch with him. We could leave the school for lunch if we had a car and could get around, so he and I headed out one day and grabbed a hamburger. From that first half hour we hung out together, there was this great connection. Brian's mom had passed away while he was in high school, and it seemed like he didn't have any buddies to chat with about it. For whatever reason, over soda and a burger, I came off as someone who wanted to do more than drink beer and talk about girls. I don't know what signaled I was one of the dudes who would talk about serious crap, but he got that right away. At least, I could *listen* about serious crap. I didn't want to talk about myself too much, and Brian didn't ask much. Over the next couple of years, Brian and I would just hang out at his house, swim in the pool, and talk. Talk talk talk. Even if I was hiding a permanent secret, with Brian, getting into some other deep shit about life felt good.

Truth is, when I first met Brian I thought he was an attractive guy. That may have been one of the reasons I was cool with being his friend, but by about the third time we hung out, any attraction I had to him had disappeared, replaced by this great friendship. Even if I had continued to find Brian attractive, it wouldn't have mattered. He was the straightest guy I'd ever met, and I was just thrilled to have a new friend in the in-crowd.

On the field, when I moved to varsity my junior year, I was steamrolling people. I was already six foot four and over three hundred pounds. There wasn't a defensive lineman we went up against who could match me pound-for-pound. I was also quick on my feet, one of the marks of a great offensive lineman. When you combine my size with my quickness, in a high school game in Shasta County, there was no stopping me or the running back behind me. The coaches made up this play with an overload formation, called "O'Callaghan Right" or "O'Callaghan Left." The other team knew what was coming and they couldn't stop it. We ran it twenty times that year, and we scored just about twenty touchdowns with it.

Both sports and hard work came naturally to me.

When I was a kid, almost all I knew about my dad's past was that he was a professional baseball player and had played in the San Francisco Giants system for a while. His example gave me a lot of confidence playing sports. The idea of playing professional sports was in our family lineage. In high school, even as I was being recruited by some major college football programs, I wasn't thinking too much about the NFL. But the possibility of following in my dad's footsteps was somewhere in the recesses of my mind. It wasn't until years later that I found out that Dad never actually played in a Major League Baseball game. He had maybe made it to a farm team for a couple seasons, but an injury derailed his career before it could get started. Regardless of where his skills actually took him, he was a good athlete, as were many of the people in my extended family. Sports were a part of us.

I also got my work ethic from my dad. He was the hardest-working person I knew. Working when he was twelve to support his family, he learned at a young age that hard work was an inherent part of life, and he passed that on to me at an equally young age.

When I was five, my dad was working at a lumber mill when he got a call one night that there was a problem with one of the boilers, so he went down to the mill to fix it. With my dad perched on top, the boiler blew up. He caught on fire and had to jump two stories to get away from the explosion. He got fried. He ended up in the burn unit for weeks, getting skin grafts on his legs and his arms. A lot of people would have slapped a big fat lawsuit on the lumber mill, but not my dad. Insurance paid the medical bills, and he was content with having those covered and heading back to work as soon as possible. I think he truly loved to work.

The only time I ever saw him was at dinner, and he missed some of those. In addition to running the mill, he was selling real estate and officiating the football games in the fall, in part for enjoyment and in part to scrape together money to keep food on the table.

My dad was always trying to get ahead, but never quite getting there. Some of his cousins were getting rich selling real estate in San Francisco, which is why he decided to try his hand at doing so around Redding. My dad was always working extra to pay the bills in Redding, yet I never felt there was something I needed that I couldn't have. We always had a place to live, always had food on the table. My dad did everything he could to make sure we kids never felt like we were struggling financially as a family, even if we were barely staying afloat back then. After all the struggles he saw his family go through when he was a kid, it meant something to him to protect us from that.

Even in that tough financial spot, he was the kind of guy who would give you the proverbial shirt off his back. And he did, all the time. If a buddy hit hard times, my dad was there. At birthdays, my dad made sure my mom had the money to get something memorable for us kids. Heck, he was a football referee, and none of them get paid what they should to take the abuse they get. My dad was a generous guy who loved to laugh, and because of that people loved being around him. I took note of that as a kid. When you gave of yourself to other people, when you opened up your wallet to them without asking for anything in return, they found a way to ignore shortcomings and get along. That stuck with me.

Like so many guys in his generation, he ended most nights with some whiskey. He would start in with the Black Velvet some time around dinner, and once he had a couple he would often start in on my mom. It sometimes seemed like everything she did was a problem. At the time I didn't understand it, and it scared the hell out of me, even though my dad never got physical with my mom. My dad never hit us kids either, but he was the enforcer of the family. He would often let out all of his frustration from the day on us.

When my dad's mom died, and she left her entire estate to my sister and me, skipping my dad, it didn't help matters. She had, by all accounts, been a terrible mother. My father told stories of her putting her cigarette out on him when he was a kid. That's some really sick stuff.

As I grew into my teens, I came to resent my dad for the way he treated my mom at night. I was a mama's boy for sure. With dad gone so much when I was a kid, I bonded a lot more with her. While my dad continued to raise his voice at my mom, I lost more and more respect for him. That drove a wedge between us that got in the way of our relationship as I became a teenager. My dad and I talked less as resentment grew inside me. I could take him yelling at me, but in my mind my mom didn't deserve any of it.

The wedge between my parents that was growing nightly built a deepening depression in me as a young kid. I knew what divorce was, and I figured our house was exactly what it looked like. It seemed inevitable that I would soon watch my dad move out as my sister and I were suddenly cast in the middle of a back-and-forth between their two lives. It ate at me. Yet despite all of the screaming matches, they somehow stayed together. I realize now that through all of that, I learned the importance of commitment. Despite their struggles in those stressful years, they had committed to marriage years before, and no series of arguments was going to upend that. They say what doesn't kill you makes you stronger. Watching their commitment, as it seemed they wanted to kill one another, actually made my understanding of ideas like commitment and loyalty a lot stronger.

As I left the house and ventured into my own career, some of my resentment for my dad turned into respect. I began to understand how his struggles had driven him to the drinking and the yelling. He had gone through hell in his life. There were lots of times he could have quit, abandoned his family, or given back less to the people around him. He never did. He just kept working hard, putting food on the table, and making his friends feel good about themselves. Years later, as my body began to hurt, I realized where my dad was coming from. I would follow in his footsteps, finding peace in a bottle. I would eventually learn that being an adult was a lot harder than it looked.

By the end of my junior year at Enterprise High School, football offers were pouring into the house. Washington, Nebraska, Cal. I knew that my size was getting me by in high school football, but in major college football I would be locked up against guys the same size. Some of them bigger. Some of them quicker. So I turned myself into a student of the game. I never liked football, but I came to understand it as well as any of my coaches. I would study the playbook religiously. I'd watch as much film as I could.

I got invited to participate in a camp at Cal by the head coach for the Golden Bears, Tom Holmoe. I had done some regional all-star games and showcases over the previous year, but this was my chance to go up against some of the best from across the country. These weren't sub-six-feet defensive linemen from Shasta County; these were big boys from across the state and some from across the country. Some of them were my size. And some of them had my strength or close to it. None of them had my quick feet. A lot of people don't realize that an offensive tackle's feet and legs can be as big a part of his success as any other aspect of his game. That was true for me.

This all got tested in one very scripted moment at the camp. There was another tackle there, a guy named Ed Blanton, who was just breaking guys. Near the end of the camp the coaching staff set up a series of battles royale, where guys went up against one another one-on-one, surrounded by all the campers, to see who could out-muscle whom. After a while Ed and I got paired up.

We both got into our three-point stances, lined up like a couple battering rams. The other campers were screaming and cheering all around us. When we got the green light, BOOM! We slammed into each other, two 300-plus-pounders using every pound to overpower the other guy. My feet made the difference as I made a move and slammed him to the ground.

When I followed that up with pancaking the best defensive lineman at the camp, that set everybody off hollering and cheering me on. On that last day they gave me the award for the best offensive lineman at the camp. The O-line coach was Ed White, who's in a bunch of halls of fame. Getting that award under the guidance of a guy like that opened my eyes a bit. I always thought I was pretty good for Northern California.

Maybe I'm better than I think.

My parents picked me up from the camp, and my dad was firing off questions for the entire three-hour drive home. Me playing college football was a dream for him. He loved football, always had. So he was dying to know how I'd done, who was my toughest competition, what did the coaches say. I gave him a couple stories, showed him the award I won. Then when we got home, I went into my bedroom, shut the door, and flopped down on the bed. All I could think about by then was a nap. Not a minute later the phone rang. My dad raced to grab it. A few seconds after, he burst into my room.

"Get on the phone!" He didn't sound excited, but rather stern. I lumbered into the living room, still sore from camp. Even when you have as good a weekend as I had on the field, the joints take a beating. I reached down and picked up the receiver.

"Ryan, Coach Holmoe." I always chuckled when I heard his

name, like he was saying "Coach Homo." He had to be a strong man to get to where he was with a name like that. Kind of like "Dick Butkus." With the insanity he must have had to deal with as a kid, he was either going to get his ass kicked . . . or become a Pro Football Hall of Famer. "How you feeling?" he asked.

"Like a million bucks, Coach." I sat on the couch to get off my aching feet.

"Great to hear, Ryan. Hell of a camp you had down here. How you feel about it?"

"You know, always room to improve." By now, telling people what they wanted to hear was second nature.

"That's the kind of attitude we can use at the University of California, Ryan. I'm calling today to ask you if you'd like to become a Golden Bear with us."

I looked at my dad, pacing a couple yards away, watching me like his life depended on it.

"Blue is my color, Coach."

We exchanged a few more pleasantries, he explained the signing process, told me to ignore other offers, cancel recruiting trips, and all that shit. Lots of him talking, lots me saying, "Yes, Coach" and "Thank you, Coach."

When I hung up that phone I knew I was going to Cal. It was too perfect, just a few hours from home and a good school. Plus, there was a liberal vibe to Cal. I was a pretty conservative guy, and being surrounded by a bunch of bleeding-heart liberals was going to be a change of pace, but I also knew that as a gay guy trying to find his way, it was better to be in Berkeley than College Station. Even though I wouldn't be coming out to anyone, I still knew the environment at Berkeley would make me hate myself a little less than a lot of other places.

Most of all, it was going to be a blessing to enter my senior season with no scholarship to play for. No pressure. Just win and have fun. I knew I'd never again have the chance to play football without feeling like there was a gun to my head to perform.

When I stood up from the couch, my dad stopped pacing. The recruiting process had just started eight to ten months earlier, and my dad had loved every minute of it. He was acting as my manager, like so many parents do. Being right in the middle of a big-time college recruiting process was heaven for him.

"I guess it's over, Dad." I shook my head and pursed my lips. "I'm going to Cal."

He stepped forward and wrapped his arms around me. He'd done it plenty of times before, but this one felt different, like he meant it more than the other times. He gripped me, then pulled back and looked me in the eye.

"I'm proud of you, son." It felt good to hear that from a guy who often seemed to prefer lots of yelling in the house.

He couldn't wait to tell my mom, who thought it was "nice," then it was a range of phone calls to his cousins and friends. I watched him for an hour, sharing this incredible pride in me with everyone he could get hold of. I never played football to make my dad proud. That just wasn't a driving force behind it. But it was also really nice to have something we shared in common, and something that he could, yes, be proud of. My dad and I had lots of differences that we didn't mind expressing, but watching him beam that day, making phone calls to his buddies, put a smile on my face.

What would he tell his buddies if he knew his son was a gay Golden Bear?

Over the coming weeks, as word got out that I had accepted an offer to Cal, attention from other schools only escalated. My dad ate it up, his son the hot-prospect football player. USC, Oregon, Florida, Texas A&M. Once you verbally accept an offer to one Power Five school, they all want you. It's like getting into the popular clique. If one of the members sits with you at lunch, everyone else suddenly wants to sit with you too. It was nice knowing I'd be sitting with the popular kids for the next few years.

Chapter 2: The Beard

My senior year of high school was simultaneously a breeze and one of the toughest years of my life. By then guys were hooking up with girls all the time. Before that, just being in the popular football clique and nearing three hundred pounds had been enough in my head to keep people's suspicions at bay. By my senior season, I was big man on campus. I would actually say, out loud, "I'm big man on campus." My mean streak was hitting its stride, and by senior year I felt the need to become a full-fledged asshole. The psychological hoops we jump through as closeted gay men are truly sick. Here's how my thinking went.

The gay guys were always the nice guys. Easy to not be that guy. They were also always the pushovers, the kids you picked on, the kids who wouldn't fight back. Again, easy to not be the pushover. Yet my fear was so deep, so all-consuming, that it wasn't enough to not be the nice guy, or not be the pushover. I had to be the raging asshole. I had this one stunt I'd pull where I would just pick a line in the hallway of the high school and walk pretty fast down that straight line. If somebody was in my way that was their problem, not mine. I never actually hurt anybody. I never wanted to go that far, and the only person I ever really wanted to hurt was myself. But I would bump into people, make them move—my way of saying, *Don't fuck with me.*

I also prided myself on my brutal honesty. I would tell people that I couldn't help but be completely honest, no matter what it was about. And I took pride in making it brutal. I hated your shirt? I told you it was ugly and you looked ugly in it. Your hair was messed up one morning? I told you so all day long. I would even tell people to "stop breathing," as though they didn't deserve to live if they were around me. And I would say it with all the venom I could muster, as though I actually wanted them to stop breathing, to die.

Here I was doing everything I possibly could to keep up this lie about me being straight, at the same time torturing everyone with my "brutal honesty." It was all so fucking cruel. The real brutal truth was that I couldn't be honest about a fucking thing that had anything to do with myself.

What's even worse is that some of the younger kids would see this big, powerful football player and try to emulate me. I was suddenly the popular kid, the one other people looked up to. I was the one they were trying to be like. I had one younger friend whose personality I watched turn, just like so many other people had watched me. He idolized me. And I watched him become this total asshole to people. I would sometimes wonder if they were hiding something deep inside them, if the other assholes in life were just so fucking miserable with themselves. The heft of setting this miserable example for these kids weighed on me even then. I decided that if I ever had the chance, I would do something to turn that upside down, set a good example for kids. Yet I always figured that chance would never come.

Somehow my charade worked perfectly. The nuances I'd picked up in my youth about how people perceived gay men were spot-on. With every carefully plotted insult I planted, every swig of beer I drank, every pound I added to my waist, I was building a persona that no one could possibly expect was some gay guy. As far as I know, no one in high school ever suspected

I was gay, and looking back I don't know how they could have. I made damn sure I defied every single gay stereotype they had ever seen on TV. My performance was Emmy-worthy.

Still, I was never satisfied with my act. It was a constant struggle to keep upping the ante, taking the "straight Ryan O'Callaghan" character to a new level. My ears were constantly perked up, listening to and overanalyzing every word my friends said around me. If my mind twisted something someone said to sound like suspicion of me being a fag, they got the full brunt of the worst of me, and I redoubled my efforts to act as "straight" as humanly possible. It was a sick existence, but it was the only way I could survive.

It wasn't until senior prom that my whole act would get put to the test. It was easy for me to just skip junior prom instead of trying to find a date I couldn't have cared less about. All of my buddies had dates to the junior prom, and I didn't want to go alone, so I just stayed home. Nobody batted an eye. Plus, I was on the young side, still sixteen at the time, so it simply wasn't a big deal to sit it out. After all, junior prom was a sideshow.

Senior prom was the main attraction. Skipping senior prom would have raised eyebrows, turned heads, and brought on a whole hell of a lot of questions. You just don't skip senior prom, especially when you're a star player on the football team headed to Cal. And you also don't go alone. I had to find a date, but frankly, I had no idea how to do that. I'd never asked a girl on a date. Ever. Even during football season I started feeling the pressures of finding a date. As the winter turned to spring of my senior year, anxiety built inside me. Seemingly everyone was declaring who they were taking to prom.

Maybe if I wait long enough, all the girls will be taken.

My buddy Karl finally came through with a recommendation: ask his girlfriend's friend Haley, and the four of us could all go together. Popping the question in the hallway between classes the next day was one of the most awkward moments of my life. Still with the asshole aura about me, I walked up to her, sweat collecting on my face, and just blurted it out.

"Hey, so you want to go to prom?" The way I said it was almost rude, like it was a complete imposition on me to have to ask her. I imagine the only reason she said yes was to hang out with her friend that night. I spent a lot of the next few weeks mapping out a master plan. Everyone knew what went on after senior prom, with couples hooking up left and right. I didn't want to have anything to do with that, but if the opportunity presented itself, my cover would be blown if I didn't take it. Since we weren't dating and we barely knew each other, I figured she wasn't going to be putting the moves on me, but I couldn't risk it. So I crafted a plan to "get sick" at some point early at the after-party so I could go home and avoid any hook-up with Haley. That way everybody would be spared a headache.

We weren't at the prom more than half an hour before Haley tugged on my arm. We had gone out to dinner with a few other couples before the big event, and suddenly Haley wasn't feeling well. Something from dinner was turning her stomach upside down. Over the course of the prom she had to excuse herself from the dance floor a few times, finally waving the white flag. I took her home and ended her night early. I felt like an asshole driving to the after-party by myself, almost happy that she had gotten sick. I had built up the possibility of having to sleep with her so much that I welcomed anything that would allow me to avoid that. Without any sex pressure at the after-party, I had an absolute blast, a bachelor again. Before I took her home, all I could think about was how I could avoid being with her intimately. It was a huge relief to avoid all of that mess.

* * *

It was during my senior year that I first tried pot. I'd always been pretty content sticking to beer, so it just hadn't been on my radar much. And honestly, I was mostly afraid of my dad finding out. All my life he had proudly talked about having never smoked anything in his life. It was a big deal to him: no cigarettes, no weed.

I had always been the good kid. My dad talked a big game about grounding us or taking away our phones or our cars. But he never had to go through with any of it because my sister and I were so well-behaved. If he found out I smoked pot, I wasn't sure exactly what his first move would be. And that was just about the last thing I ever wanted to find out. So I stayed out of trouble and stayed away from pot.

In Chico I went with Brian and a couple friends to watch our basketball team in a tournament my senior year. I never played basketball, and frankly, I never had much interest in even watching our own team. But a guy on the Chico team was having a big party one night of the tournament, so we went down to check it out. I wouldn't be back home until the next day, so I figured the chances of my dad finding out about it were zero. A buddy had gotten a bag of weed trimmings, and he was eager to try it out. He hadn't smoked much then either, or he probably would have skipped the trimmings. The pot people usually smoke is actually the bud of the marijuana plant. To get to the good stuff, you have to trim away a bunch of leaves and shit, and then you're left with what you actually want to smoke. This bag was full of the stuff that was left discarded on the floor. It was low potency, but I was game.

In our friend's car in front of that party in Chico, sitting in the front seat, I lit up for the first time. I passed the joint to one of my buddies and leaned back in the seat.

"It might take a minute to kick in," he said.

After a couple minutes I didn't feel a thing, so I asked for another hit. And then a few minutes later, another. I'm not sure I felt a thing the whole night. Take my size and add to it some barely potent pot and you have a recipe for a dud. If that was all pot did, I certainly didn't want to risk my dad's wrath over it. I may have smoked two more times my entire senior year, and that was just to continue to fit in with the guys. In my head, pot was a straight-dude thing. And many of the straight dudes I knew were dabbling in it at parties. I didn't want to stand out as different in any way, so I went along with it. As long as my dad didn't find out, it was just another great way to keep my cover.

Even with my success at the Cal camp, I never truly believed I could play high-level football until one of my final games, against Pleasant Valley High School. Their quarterback was a junior, a kid named Aaron Rodgers.

I'd woken up that day with a terrible flu. Sick to my stomach. It was the biggest game at Enterprise High School in a while, and I was the best player on the team. No chance I was going to miss it. Late in the game we were up by a touchdown and I finally tapped out. I'd been vomiting throughout the game but holding my own. I played both sides of the line that season, and that game was no different. After forty-six minutes of play, I just couldn't go.

As I stuck my head in a trash can on the sideline, Rodgers was doing his thing. Completion. Handoff, first down. Completion. Another first down. When I looked up from the trash, time was winding down and Rodgers had moved Pleasant Valley into scoring position. It was third down and they took their last time-out.

My position coach walked over to me. "Ryan, how you—"

I brushed past him, putting on my helmet, trudging out

to the field. Rodgers and I had become friendly in high school, seeing one another at games and the occasional party. We were two of the biggest football names in the area.

I am not losing this game to Aaron fucking Rodgers.

I headed out onto the field, a bit wobbly. Because the time-out was almost over, and I was a late substitution, a funny thing happened: nobody on the other team noticed I was there. It was third and two, so a handoff made all the sense in the world when my backup was in. Oops.

BOOM! I grabbed the running back by the shoulder and slammed him to the ground. Fourth down.

The clock was moving. Twenty . . . nineteen . . . eighteen . . . No time-outs. The clock would stop after this play no matter what, so they just needed a few yards for first down. They moved an additional tight end to my side; I knew a double-team was coming. The question was whether it was going to be a run or a pass. With fourth and short, you figure run. But with a guy like Rodgers, he could pass, keep the ball, whatever.

Looking at the formation, the tackle was shoulder-to-shoulder with the guard, and the tight end was no deeper.

Idiots.

I barked to my teammates to clue them in on the run call. "HIKE!"

I pushed the tight end off me for a moment and watched the runner. Were they really running my way?

Idiots.

There was no way I could actually get to the runner before he rounded the corner, so I just used the tackle as a battering ram and slammed him into the guy. The ball carrier bounced off him and hesitated long enough for one of my teammates to grab him for another loss.

Game. Over.

I stood over those guys as my teammates rushed onto the field. As people celebrated, all I could think about was how I dominated another game. At the biggest moment of the biggest game of my high school career, with me sick as a dog, I walloped these guys. On both sides of the ball.

"Good game," Aaron said as we did the handshake-hug at midfield. "Good luck at Cal."

"Come join me," I said.

He smiled. He was a good high school quarterback, but he wasn't getting many looks from Division I schools. He knew he wouldn't be playing in the Pac-10 anytime soon.

I would be. Everyone else around me had been telling me for two years how good I was, but I had always felt they just couldn't see past Podunk Redding. I was bigger, stronger, and smarter than every opponent in my small-town area of NoCal. I had gotten a glimpse at the Cal camp, though I still found reasons in my head to doubt myself even after that. But in that game I finally saw it too. For the first time.

I could be a star.

What's more, I could keep wearing football as my "beard" for years to come. I'm not sure where exactly the term "beard" came from originally, but it's slang for a woman who goes on a date with a gay guy to make him appear to be straight. Some gay guys even marry women as their "beards" to keep up appearances. For me, football would be the date on my arm that told everyone, *That guy is 100 percent certifiably straight.* There are lots of other macho sports out there, but none of them carry the aura of tough-guy straightness that football has. It's the perfect beard for a gay guy trying to hide.

I needed a beard to live. By the end of high school I had realized I could never exist as a gay man. Coming out, dating guys, none of that would ever be accepted by anyone in my life.

My parents would disown me. My friends would reject me. I would be disinvited from every family picnic for the rest of my life. The handful of gays in Redding were outcasts, mocked and ridiculed incessantly. No matter where I ended up in life, there was absolutely no way I could be an openly gay man, or even have secret sex with another guy.

I also decided I could never marry a woman. I simply had no interest in sleeping with a woman, I had no interest in living with a woman, I had no interest in being the partner of a woman. Don't get me wrong, I had some close female friends. One of Brian's girlfriends, Starr, was awesome. She would be one of my biggest supporters for years to come. And I absolutely adored my mother. I loved her more than I loved anyone else in the world, including myself. But walking down the aisle with a woman, committing to a life with her, was something I had no interest in. And because of that, I couldn't do that to a woman. I knew I could never give a woman everything she wanted and needed in a husband. It would be a marriage of convenience, of *my* convenience, not of happiness or love.

Yet eventually I would have to either marry a woman or come out. Guys like me weren't single into their thirties or forties without everyone assuming they're gay. I couldn't have that. I had one great uncle who was single all his life, my mom's uncle. He lived along the Russian River by himself, hording all kinds of junk while fishing the river for dinner. He was an "artist" who had made some sort of living painting billboards back in the day. I saw him only a handful of times throughout my childhood. Once was at my grandmother's house for Thanksgiving. He stayed mostly to himself, talking only to my grandma and maybe a couple siblings. I never spoke to him, but I watched him that day, how he moved sheepishly, like he didn't belong with his family at Thanksgiving. Much like my picnics among the redwoods. Looking back now, I get melancholy thinking about the life he felt he had to live, even closer to San Francisco than I was, and the life he could have lived.

As long as I played football, it would be my beard masking my loneliness. Busting my ass to succeed at the most popular sport in America was going to be a lot of work. If I could continue to graduate to the next level of this sport, as macho of a sport as it was, I would keep my cover.

During my senior season, what spun around in my head was what to do after football. I owned my first rifle when I was just twelve. Guns were a part of my life. They were in our house, in my closet, and I knew how to use them. I had been trained at a very young age how to care for a firearm, how to use it correctly, and how to defend myself with it. My father taking me on hunting excursions was only part of my exposure to guns. Their presence in our lives was part and parcel of being an O'Callaghan. I figured even before I got to Cal that some day, when football was over, I'd need to take one of those guns and put a bullet in my head.

I guess some people talk about killing themselves in broad terms and never really mean it. I meant it. I didn't want to die, to be sure. Graduating from high school, the way I looked at it, Cal football would keep me alive for the next five years. I'd get everything I possibly could out of the experience. I'd have as much fun as I could while always looking over my shoulder. And then it would all be over.

Chapter 3: Award-Winning Performance

It was really easy to hide at Cal. When I got there nobody knew who I was other than a big football player from Redneck Country who could probably break you in half. There wasn't a reason on earth for anyone at that school to suspect I was gay. Hell, there was every reason to think I wasn't. Still, it was always on my mind, even more than when I was in high school. In high school I was king of the locker room. I held court in the veterans' part of the locker room and poked fun at the younger players whenever I wanted. Plus, nobody ever felt the pressure to take a shower. I never took a shower after practice or a game in high school.

At Cal I was suddenly the low man on the depth chart, not even playing as a redshirt my first year. And the guys showered after practice and after games. I didn't feel comfortable being naked around the guys, so I always found a reason to delay my shower, strip down, and rinse off after most or all of the other guys were done. The whole new dynamic of my new team and my new locker room forced my mind into a new dilemma, like I had to create my character all over again.

So I started chewing tobacco, which was popular on the team. Gay guys smoked tobacco, they didn't chew it. The tobacco chewers were guy's guys. They wore cowboy hats and played sports. They were big, strong guys nobody messed with. I also

45

drank lots more beer, even more than I ever did in high school. Whenever possible at a social event, even at eighteen years old, I had a beer can in my hand.

As soon as I got to Cal I also became aware that I had buddies around all the time. I didn't go home to my parents' house at night, I was now sleeping in the bedroom next to my teammates. They saw my every move, and they saw everyone who went in and out of my bedroom. It didn't take long before they were having nighttime visitors, and I figured I was going to have to do the same. It wasn't going to be difficult. Being a big-time football player on campus, the women would hit on me plenty. I may have been big and fat, but the women didn't mind. They liked the idea of a big, strong guy who could protect them. Guys are obsessed with bodies. Women, it seemed to me then, wanted somebody who would be good to them and care for them. I felt shitty that I was going to have to use some of them to keep up appearances with my buddies, but I figured they were using me for something too. And I had to do it.

One afternoon my freshman year I was hanging out with the offensive line, drinking pitchers of cheap beer at a popular college watering hole in Berkeley. I wasn't twenty-one, but as long as an upperclassman was doing the ordering and getting the glasses, nobody asked questions of the six-foot-six, three-hundred-pound eighteen-year-old. It was still early and pretty dead in there, and we were just shooting the shit, when an attractive, tall blond woman walked in the door all alone.

Everybody at the table watched her strut her stuff across the floor. One of the things I noticed about the Cal football team early on was that the "fag" and "gay" comments were thrown around by the guys a lot less than in high school. That outward homophobic language just wasn't there much in college. What replaced it was even more overt straightness. Guys talked about girls in high school, but in college it was an obsession. I wasn't sure which one was worse for me. The "fag" stuff was almost dismissible as kids being stupid. The constant "girls girls girls" mantra in college put me on a whole new island by myself. It was a reminder every few minutes—and yes, that's how often some comment about girls and sex would come up with the guys—that I was different, and that I wouldn't be welcome if I was a queer.

Time for me to step up.

She went to the bar and ordered a glass of white wine. The guys were still ogling her, twittering quietly. After she got her glass of wine, she turned around and immediately made her way over to me.

"Is this seat taken?" she asked, not waiting for an answer before she proceeded to sit on my lap. Again, it was early and the place was pretty empty. There were countless empty chairs all around us, but she chose my lap. I actually thought in those first moments that I was being set up by the other guys. I thought my teammates suspected I was gay, and this was their way of putting me to the test. Little did they know that I had been studying for this test every day for years. Lying in bed at night, or in the morning before getting up, or driving around town, I would go over every possible scenario in my mind of how I would react if I were a straight guy. I thought if I acted awkward, hesitated in any way, my cover would be blown. I had to be prepared for the test—I had to ace it. All the studying I'd done, watching how straight guys act, move, talk, and spinning all of that in my head, came to bear that Saturday afternoon.

It's showtime.

As soon as she sat on my lap, I immediately put my hand on her waist, just like I had rehearsed a thousand times in my head. She did absolutely nothing for me, but I had seen my straight buddies do it, so that's what I did. I could feel her react to my touch, settling comfortably onto my lap. Whatever I did, it worked. She didn't leave my lap for a couple hours, all of us laughing and talking the whole time. Our beer pitchers and her wineglass stayed full.

With each passing minute of her putting her arms around my neck, grabbing my legs, I knew this was going to finally be the night I had to get with a woman for the first time. If she had just said hello and went on her way, or even stopped by for a single drink, it would have been easy to tell the other guys it just didn't work out with her. But this young woman was throwing herself at me, not moving from my lap for two hours. Not sealing the deal would have been an impossible result to explain to my buddies. I had convinced myself that they would be getting a report from her the next day, and if I didn't get naked with her, I was done for. Not many straight guys would pass up the chance to have sex with her. She was really pretty and she was giving me every opportunity. If football is the maker of men in America, sex with women is what defines them to one another.

When it was time to go, I made sure everyone saw us leaving together. If she ran away from me screaming, I wanted them to at least see my effort. She didn't run away. Without ever saying what we were going to do, we naturally wandered the streets back to my place. She stayed the night until leaving early the next morning before breakfast.

Some people have asked me over the last few years how I knew I was gay. I just knew. Even before having sex with another person, all of my fantasies and desires involved other guys. My eyes never lingered on a woman the way they did with a good-looking guy. I never longed to spend time with a cute girl the way I did with a cute guy. You don't need to have sex with people to know whom you want to have sex with. Even before

I ever had sex, I knew what I wanted. That night, sleeping with a woman for the first time, confirmed my theory beyond any shadow of a doubt: I was gay gay gay.

Yet leaving the bar with that one person that one time, and bringing her home with me, bought me a couple years of cover with my friends. I was a straight guy in their minds, no questions asked.

Still, I didn't leave it there. The paranoia about people discovering my secret was constant. I had to continue working at keeping up my straight veneer. That woman might have been the first I had sex with, but she wasn't the last. Whenever I did it, I made sure it was at the perfect opportunity for other people to see me. It wasn't worth it if I had sex with a woman and no one knew it. After parties, connecting at a local bar, the moments were few and far between, but it was enough to keep up appearances.

Speaking of appearances, I let mine go. Gay guys were waiflike twinks with perfect haircuts and six-packs who dressed like they were modeling for a catalog. At Cal I became a total slob. I gained dozens of pounds, tipping the scales as high as 370. At one point my teammate Marshawn Lynch dubbed me "Baby Huey" after the big, fat, naive cartoon character. That name cracked him up. He wasn't far off. My coaches didn't like the obesity at all. They told me that some heft is key for an offensive lineman, but I had gone overboard. Not only did it undermine my mobility, but it was downright unhealthy, and it would make recovering from any kind of injury I might suffer a lot more difficult. I didn't care.

I also dressed the part. My daily attire for class was mostly big, baggy Cal-sponsored sweatshirts and workout pants that were oversized even for my fat ass. They were perfect for my class-time bridge between my morning workouts and afternoons at the stadium. And they were super comfortable. When you're carrying around an extra 150 pounds, you just want to be as comfortable as possible. If I didn't have football duties it was generally a huge oversized white T-shirt and jeans. None of this was any different from most of the varsity athletes, men and women, walking or riding their bikes around campus. The bigger I got, and the worse I dressed, the more I'd blend into the scenery and the less likely anyone would connect me to *Will & Grace.*

The other added benefit? Women were also less likely to check me out. Don't get me wrong, a lot of women really like to be with a huge guy. But at the same time, at 370 pounds I did not have girls banging at my door the way a lot of the more fit wide receivers and quarterbacks did. Being obese, it was a lot easier to explain a "forced celibacy" than it would have been if I was some hot, fit linebacker.

All of this left me in a common state of loneliness and depression that built through the first four years at Cal. With constant worrying about what people said, how to respond, when to chew tobacco, how to look, act, and feel like I was someone I wasn't, there wasn't much energy left for positivity. There were many times when I was overcome with emotion. I would sometimes cry in bed as my mind spun out of control. The natural response when you hold a bunch of stuff in is that it comes out in spurts of emotion and tears. Of course, I had to carefully manage those spurts. I was a big, tough straight guy. I didn't feel emotions like sadness. Tears were not supposed to fall from my face.

It was in my first Cal spring game that the dreaded injury bug first hit. I dropped back into pass coverage and got a hand on the defensive end. The problem was, I also got two fingers on him, which got caught in his jersey. When he blasted past my right shoulder, he took those two fingers with him, bending them back so far that they touched my forearm. *Snap!* I knew as soon as I felt it that something had gone terribly wrong. Trying to peel the glove off my hand on the sideline was excruciating. I hadn't felt pain like that before, and I haven't since. It was like someone was taking a steak knife and sawing into my knuckles. When the glove came off, I had to use my other hand to hold up my middle and ring fingers. Sure enough, the X-ray confirmed it: both metacarpal bones had completely snapped in half. Spring football was over for me.

Surgery was scheduled for a few days later. I had never had surgery before, so I was a little nervous to go under the knife. I also had no clue of what to expect. The night before the surgery I was a bit on edge. Chase Lyman, one of the receivers on the team who eventually played for the New Orleans Saints, invited me to go hang out with him, quarterback Kyle Boller, and a couple other guys at Kyle's place. Poker and beer. It sounded great to me. Hanging out with them that night really took my mind off the impending surgery. The beer didn't hurt either. I drank a lot that night, and this was completely intentional. By the time I left Kyle's place, my impending surgery was barely a thought in my mind.

As soon as I came to after surgery the next day, lying there on the gurney in the recovery room, I was puking all over the place. And I mean *all over*. It came suddenly, and it was quickly covering me, on my sheets, on the floor. It went on and on for a while. When the doc had asked me before surgery if I'd had any alcohol the night before, I didn't think much of the question and downplayed just how much I had drunk. Now I understood why he was asking. Between vomit explosions I was regretting my fun poker night more and more.

Why didn't anyone tell me about this?

Chase, Kyle, and I got a couple good laughs out of that one, and how dumb I had been. They were more seasoned and knew that with every swig of beer I was digging a bigger hole for myself the next day. They were perfectly cool with letting me find out all on my own what a little alcohol does with anesthesia. I didn't mind. Hell, it made me feel good about where I was with the guys. Bearing the brunt of a prank, or being teased by the guys about something I did or a little quirk I carried, meant I was part of the crew. And I was desperate to be part of the crew. It was all meant in good fun and to make me feel at home. As long as the teasing didn't have anything to do with sex or any hint about being gay, I was glad to be on the receiving end of it, knowing that in a couple years I'd be dishing it out myself.

Still, I never made that mistake again. After that whole incident I became painfully aware of every presurgery restriction known to medics. That hand, now sporting five screws, has bothered me ever since. It would prove to be the first in a long series of war scars from the trenches of the gridiron.

My second major injury came after my second playing season, which was my redshirt sophomore year. This time during spring ball I injured my left shoulder. When the doctor took a good look at it over the summer, he said I had torn the labrum. We elected to forgo the surgery until after the next season, which meant lots of injections to the shoulder to quell the pain, and some painkillers for good measure. That was the first time I started using painkillers on a basis beyond a brief surgery recovery. But if you've ever had a torn labrum, you know there's no way an offensive lineman could have that injury and block oncoming defenders without something to kill the pain. The pills were, at the time, a necessary evil. After that season I got the surgery, my second in as many years.

During my redshirt junior year, I injured both shoulders and required two more surgeries. It was the last season for Aaron Rodgers, who had transferred to Berkeley in 2003 (more on this shortly), and our running back, J.J. Arrington. I certainly wasn't going to miss any of that season because of some dumb surgery. After the season they repaired one shoulder, and then they went in for the other one as soon as I could wipe my own ass.

Following my senior season I needed left-shoulder surgery again. It was my fifth surgery in just four years, and managing pain became a routine part of life for me. Through all of it, my coaches implored me to lose weight. They had warned me about a prolonged and ineffective recovery with every pound over 330 I let myself get. It was all lost on me. Far more important to me than an effective recovery and rehab period was continuing my charade of the big, fat, sloppy straight guy. So that those guys around me at age twenty would always think I was straight, I risked my long-term health for the rest of my life. Given that I never planned to live past thirty, it seemed like a good trade-off at the time.

Coach Holmoe never coached me in a game. After my redshirt year, he was canned. We had gone 1–10 and finished last in the conference. Nobody was surprised when he was let go. Beyond the shitty record he put up at Cal, his personality just didn't fit the program. He was a funny guy who loved to give speeches. Oh, the speeches. One day at camp in Turlock, a farming community about a hundred miles east of Berkeley, he gathered us under a tree and waxed poetic about the team being a tree and all the players its branches. He was getting emotional as he talked, and the guys made fun of him for it long after the speech was over. That was the first and only head-coaching gig he had.

Holmoe ended up the athletic director at Brigham Young

University. He was a devout Mormon. I never gave it much thought, me being gay and him being Mormon. To me, a Christian was probably going to hate me for being gay whether he was Mormon, Catholic, or Protestant, so it didn't matter much. Add in "football coach" and you had the double whammy.

When Jeff Tedford came to the program, I was nervous and excited. The last thing I wanted to do was play for a team that won one game in a season. Yet with a new coach could come personnel changes, his own recruits. I wasn't going to lose my scholarship anytime soon, so I wasn't worried about that. But you never know what can happen. That year I got some playing time and we beat two top-25 teams. A winning record was a new concept for the team, and we were all excited about the next few years.

But the best was yet to come. My second year at Cal I hosted a recruiting trip for Aaron Rodgers. Coming out of high school he hadn't found much interest from the big-time schools, so he settled on Butte College, a community college not far from his hometown of Chico. Coach Tedford had caught wind of a tight end from Butte, Garrett Cross, and he glimpsed the guy throwing passes to Garrett on the scouting film he got in the mail. When he went to scout Cross he saw Aaron up close and in person. Aaron had put up some big numbers at his junior college that year, so the team brought him to Berkeley for a few days. I was excited to play host that weekend, and by the possibility of a guy I knew and had played against joining the team.

Aaron was typical Aaron on that recruiting trip. He has a signature off-kilter sense of humor that makes people fall in love with him. But gosh he can be boring. On my Cal recruiting trip the guys brought me to one of the local bars, where I proceeded to drink so much that I puked in the bathroom. Aaron didn't want any of that. He never did. We went to dinner together, but there were no strippers or crazy nights you hear about on so many recruiting trips. Aaron's visit to Cal was a business trip for him. He wanted to know about Berkeley, a bit about San Francisco, and what it was like being a student-athlete at Cal. Even then, a junior-college quarterback, he was a pro's pro, keeping his personal life and good times at arm's length from his football career.

After that trip Aaron signed with Cal and joined us in Berkeley. He lived next door to a couple linemen, so I was over there all the time. We got to know each other well the two years we played together at Cal, bonding over our shared high school experiences and the increasing attention we were both getting from NFL scouts. Aaron was usually playing online poker while the rest of us drank. When he did join us for a drink, and that wasn't all too common, it was usually a wine cooler. Beer was never his thing.

On the field we were having a blast as soon as Aaron started playing. In just his second start for Cal, we were up 21–7 on USC at halftime when he had to leave the game with an injury. We still pulled out the win, handing Reggie Bush, Matt Leinart, and the Trojans their only loss of the season. That night we all went to a big party at FIJI, one of the party frats at Cal, and got hammered off our asses. A couple days later my picture ended up in *Sports Illustrated*. That was pretty cool.

My junior season was Aaron's second and last year at Cal. It was magical. This time USC returned the favor, beating us in Los Angeles 23–17, our only regular-season loss that year. It was the offense's worst performance of the season, and we all felt like crap about it. If we had been able to knock off USC, we would have played for a national championship.

Even after Aaron left, the ship kept sailing. Marshawn Lynch and Justin Forsett tag teamed to power an impressive running game, and we went on to win a bowl game my senior year.

My first two years at Cal I barely smoked pot. I might have gotten high twice freshman year in the dorms, and my second year I lived with Chase Lyman, who didn't touch the stuff. At this point I had only smoked it a few times, and frankly, it just wasn't that good. I'd gotten "bad stuff," as they say. By my third year at Cal I started smoking with some frequency. Not a lot, but I became much less averse to it.

It was those last couple years at Cal that some of the other guys really opened my eyes to it. Like I said, it helped manage the pain a lot. But the reason I had access to it all the time was because I suddenly had more money coming in than I needed. When my grandmother had died years earlier, she left me money to receive a monthly stipend. The amount increased at one point when I was at Cal, so I had extra money to spend.

I was also working as a bouncer and a security guard at frat parties and other parties in San Francisco. A bunch of the guys on the football team were doing it. It was easy money, more money than we should have been paid at the time. We were obvious choices for the job of any frat party on campus. People knew who the football players were, and because of the team's success, we had some clout around campus. Nobody was going to cross us. And if they did, chances are they weren't six foot six and 370 pounds.

Having the extra money to buy pot meant I became Mr. Popular on the team with a bunch of guys. I always had a stash in my room, and it seemed like guys were over all the time to smoke. Some of the biggest stars on the team suddenly wanted to hang out with the right tackle. We'd just sit around my living room for hours smoking, shooting the shit. The example my dad had shown me as a kid about the power of generosity was something I put into practice those last couple years at Cal. If I was generous with giving pot to my teammates, they wouldn't question me as a person, they would just accept me as the guy handing out joints. Instead of trying to figure out who I was, they would just treat me as Ryan the generous guy with the pot. Whether I was dating girls or not wouldn't even cross their minds.

This was when I first learned that pot helped with the pain of football. Sometimes it was a dull pain sitting in class, other times it stabbed me like a knife waking me up in bed. Virtually every single football player in Division I experiences some kind of troubling injury somewhere along his career. It could be a torn this or a broken that. Whatever it is, everybody in major football is looking for some way to dull the pain, often chronic pain that surgeries and prescribed painkillers simply won't put out of your mind.

As my surgeries mounted even in college, the pain of playing the game increased. The guys were only getting bigger, faster, and stronger as I moved up the depth chart. And with my hand and shoulder surgeries, plus my excessive weight, I started looking for ways to dull the pain. It's not why I started smoking, and I don't think it's why a lot of guys do. But I'll tell you this: it's why I did it more often. By my senior year, after every game the team doctor would put two Vicodin and a muscle relaxer inside a rubber glove so I could carry them home to take before bed. I didn't love it, but it was the only way to cut through the pain and get to sleep. Having access to the pot on a daily basis, and feeling how it dulled a lot of the aches and pains, was a revelation for me. It was for a lot of other guys too. It's something we talked about, how stupid it was that this drug that was helping us so much after games was illegal.

For me, the weed was all I needed. I quickly found that from the sore muscles to the broken bones to the torn ligaments, smoking pot made my entire body feel better in a way the Vicodin only masked. And I just didn't like the Vicodin they prescribed to me after surgeries. At my size, I always needed a bit more of it than the regular person, and after a few days it fucked with how my mind worked. I definitely used the prescriptions after the surgeries, but once I found pot I used that a lot more to control the pain day to day. It was safer and I just liked it more.

Pot got a lot more illegal for the football team while I was at Cal. Drug tests started at some point, and it freaked out a lot of the guys. Tedford came into a meeting one day with the big announcement, and you could hear the gasps in the room. But the school also simultaneously created a program they called "safe harbor." The concept was that if you told a team psychologist that you were doing drugs and trying to stop, the school would not hold you accountable for a positive test. However, you had to take some steps to actually get off of whatever drug you were doing. It was a way for the school to monitor who was actually doing what by offering them clemency.

I didn't hesitate to spill my guts about the pot. The last thing I needed was to lose my scholarship or any shot at playing football because I was smoking. And by then I didn't want to stop. I don't remember ever getting tested, and I don't remember any real effort to get me to stop. Hell, I don't remember *anybody* on the team ever getting tested. But it was the early days of the program, and they were just figuring it out. I'm told it's now a lot more strict. I was thankful for the leniency, but it was a reminder that people in power in sports were taking a close look at drug use. It was going to be something I would have to come face-to-face with eventually.

* * *

Another inheritance I got when I was at Cal was my grandpa's service revolver. He was a cop in San Francisco, and I always made my love of guns known to people, another way to look like a tough guy.

I took out that gun only once while I was living in Berkeley. We were all sitting around the house, I think it was my third year at Cal. We lived near a park where a bunch of homeless people spent a lot of time. This night, one of the homeless guys walked into the house. He wasn't like a lot of the other guys stumbling around and mumbling. This guy seemed to have his wits about him, standing up straight. He had a purpose.

"Nobody move," he said to the four or five of us sitting in the living room. "I got a gun."

I had just come into the room so it was easy for me to duck back into the hallway and head to my room. I doubted the guy actually had a gun, but I knew for sure that I had one. I opened my safe, grabbed my loaded revolver, and went back into the living room, pointing the gun ahead of me, ready to put a bullet in this asshole's chest. When I got there the guys were laughing their asses off.

"We told him you actually had a gun and he took off."

That little episode was good for laughs for the rest of my time at Cal.

That night by myself in my room, as I put the revolver back in the safe for security and easy access, I wondered if I actually would have shot him, this dumb-ass homeless guy thinking he could scare a bunch of college kids with a finger in his hoodie pocket. I didn't even like shooting deer, forget about shooting another person. But what bothered me about shooting a deer was its complete innocence. It wasn't doing anything to get shot, just foraging for some food and tending to its fawn. This guy was walking into a house and threatening people. Yes, I could have and would have shot him if I'd walked back in that room and he had a gun out. I was taught to never pull out a gun in a situation like that if I did not intend to use it. Thankfully, he made the decision easy.

Football is of course a team sport, and I always viewed it that way. I wanted to do my job to help the team, and figure out what I could do to support the guys around me. That's inherent in an offensive lineman. Everybody in and around college football knows the names Aaron Rodgers, Marshawn Lynch, Justin Forsett, and J.J. Arrington. But not many know Ryan O'Callaghan. That's because it's not the role of an offensive lineman to be the star, but to help the burgeoning stars *become* stars and keep them shining once they're there.

If you look at a football stats sheet, virtually every player is accounted for. The quarterback has his passer rating, the running back has his yards per carry, the defensive linemen have their sacks, and the defensive backs have their interceptions. Even the punter has his yards per punt on the stat sheet. Who are the only people who never show up in the stats? The offensive linemen. If we show up in the stats, maybe for a fumble recovery, it's because something went horribly, horribly wrong and we somehow fell on a ball before anyone else could. When do you see us? It's usually when we are penalized for holding. When we miss a block and the quarterback is sacked. You can measure an offensive lineman's success by how little his name appears in the newspapers.

Life on the line can be a really lonely place. It's also the perfect place to hide. Nobody knows your name, and because of the helmets nobody knows your face. The people who become extra important to you are the guys around you, whether they're the stars you're blocking for or the other guys on the line. The tightest group on virtually any football team is the offensive line. If we're not working together in tandem and communicating regularly, the entire offense falls apart. And because we get so few accolades from anyone outside the team, it becomes that much more important to have support from the guys next to you.

It's one of the reasons the great quarterbacks all get tight with their offensive lines. Guys like Aaron know that while his name is plastered on the headlines and his face appears in the TV commercials, a big part of that is the no-name 300-pounders standing in front of him every week.

I say all of this as a roundabout way of getting to my proudest moment with the Cal football team. Like I said, the success of the team was priorities one, two, and three for me, and it is for any offensive lineman. But on those rare occasions when we receive some praise, it certainly does feel good. By my senior season I was nearly unstoppable. In twelve games that year, I believe I gave up only one sack. That's damn good.

I was flown to Seattle late that year to attend the Morris Trophy ceremony, where I was given the award as the best offensive lineman in the Pac-10. My parents came with me, my dad beaming the whole time. The guy who won the award on the defensive side, Oregon's Haloti Ngata, whom I had actually voted for that year, was a no-show as his mother was dealing with a disease that would take her life a month later. Since I was the only winner present at the ceremony, it meant that much more attention from the media and the attendees.

I loved winning the award. I fucking hated the attention.

The most important part of the award for me is that it's not voted on by a bunch of people looking at stats. Hell, given we have no stats, it can't be. It's also not handed out by a group of reporters sitting in the press box behind their keyboards trying to whip up the next hot take that will draw a bunch of clicks. Instead, the award is voted on by the players who went up against you all season. The guys in the trenches fighting against you are the only ones whose opinions matter with the Morris Trophy. That the defensive linemen across the conference would vote for me as the best offensive lineman they went up against all season was incredibly special. It validated all of the hard work, the physical pain, and the surgeries I had endured throughout college.

It also validated my constant push to keep my sexuality far away from anyone in my life. I don't believe for a second that in 2005 I would have won that award if the other guys knew I was gay. I think that may have changed a bit since then. But back then, there's no chance that my opponents would have acknowledged that a gay guy had gotten the best of them all season long.

My personal football success during my senior year helped cut into my daily depression a lot. Shortly after Aaron got drafted the year before, he introduced me to his whole management team, including his agent and financial manager. I knew I wasn't supposed to be communicating with them at the time, but the allure of the NFL was too strong to not talk to these guys who were expressing a very real interest in my future. The potential of the NFL literally meant living several more years. If my football beard was going to continue, then ending my life would be able to wait.

These guys were so high on me that they convinced me to take out insurance on my body ahead of my senior season at Cal. I had to be catastrophically injured to cash in, but they thought it was a good idea so I went along with it. Of course, I knew there was no way I would ever collect on that policy. But when an NFL agent and financial advisor told me to do something, I did it. I figured telling them "No thanks" would have just raised questions I didn't want to answer.

Chapter 4: The Waiting Game

After my senior season I got a call from Brian wanting to reconnect. He was living in Salt Lake City at the time. I was headed to Vegas the next weekend with our quarterback, Joe Ayoob, and his girlfriend, and I invited Brian to tag along. We had barely stayed in contact when I was in college, so at first it felt a little odd for him to suddenly be a part of my life again. But he came to Vegas and spent one night with us. Like best friends so often do, we picked up right where we'd left off. After that trip we were chatting all the time like we had all those years in high school. Soon we started talking about him joining me wherever I ended up after the NFL Draft. He had a job with a cell phone company that he could probably do from anywhere else, and he loved the idea of moving out of Salt Lake City.

Having him live with me would be genius for a couple reasons. For one, I'd have somebody to help move me to wherever I ended up. I was expecting a difficult time in my new city, just because I knew being an NFL rookie would require loads of studying and workouts and long hours at the facility. Having a right-hand man like Brian would be a lifesaver.

The other thing I loved about it was that Brian was a lady-killer, always on the prowl, the ultimate "straight guy." Living with him and spending time with him would create an innocence by association. He'd have girls around the house, we'd have girls with us when we went out, and I figured I could put on enough of an act around them to look like I was interested. And he was all-in on living with me. It was the perfect scenario.

When draft day rolled around, I was nervous but excited. Everything I had done at Cal had suddenly been about preparing me to continue my football career in the pros. When I entered Cal, I figured I'd play Division I college football, graduate, and end my life. Yet the NFL offered another lease on life that I simply hadn't anticipated just a few years earlier. A lot of guys get excited for the NFL Draft because it means they'll get paid, or they'll get famous, or they'll continue playing the game they've loved all their life. I was just excited for the opportunity to keep playing my straight-football character. And with all I had done in college, a shot at the NFL seemed certain. Once you get to that level you only make it by continuing to work hard and study, but those two things were never an issue for me. Busting my ass and focusing on football kept my mind busy. I just needed a shot.

After blocking for Aaron, Marshawn, J.J., and Justin at Cal, and winning a bunch of awards and game balls along the way, various NFL teams took real interest in me. Following the last game of my senior season I started hiring people who would steer me in the right direction. As I've said, Aaron helped with a lot of that. He had already gone through the process the year before, so he had a lot of the system already set up. I just copied his blueprint, hiring a couple of the guys he'd already introduced me to—his agent and his money guy. Of course, I wasn't going to be a quarterback selected in the first round, so I probably didn't need the whole support structure he had around him. Aaron was one of the faces of the NFL Draft when he came out of college. I was doing my best to keep playing football and get as little publicity or attention as possible. But it was just so easy to do it the way Aaron had already done it.

In the weeks before the draft it was looking like I would be a second- or third-round pick. I was in a number of experts' top-10 offensive tackles that draft, and offensive linemen consistently do well in the NFL Draft. Mel Kiper, an ESPN football analyst, was giving me some love at one point on one of his lists of guys to keep an eye on. All of the people around me echoed what I had heard: first-day draft pick, from the mid-second to early-third round.

My friend Starr, Brian's girlfriend from high school, hosted a big draft party for me at her parents' house in Redding. Starr had come to a lot of my games at Cal. She was there for the big upset over USC and the crazy celebration that ensued. Because she was around a lot, some of the guys figured she and I were dating. I never lied about it, but I never cleared up the speculation either. I was thrilled to have the guys thinking I was dating a girl, and a girl they had met. She wasn't some fictitious "girlfriend back home." Starr never realized it, but she helped me keep up the charade while I was at Cal. It helped a lot.

Her parents' house was the perfect spot for the big draft-day celebration. That house belongs in a magazine. Absolutely picture-perfect with gorgeous views. Plus, it had plenty of space for all the people who wanted to join us. My grandmother came by, along with a bunch of friends from Redding. My aunt and Uncle John drove the three hours from the mountains to be there. Brian came, despite he and Starr having long since broken up.

There was even a local sports reporter there, a guy I played football with in high school. By now I had become a bit of a celebrity in town. It's not every day that a town like Redding has a hometown kid picked in the NFL Draft. The most recent had been Jason Sehorn, who was from nearby Mount Shasta. That was a dozen years earlier. When the sportswriter asked to be there for the big moment, I was excited to share it with the community.

The champagne was ready to pop, and I had my phone in my hands, constantly making sure the ringer was on, for the call I'd get. Before the draft started, Starr gave me one of my Cal jerseys framed really nicely. It was a nice final goodbye to the college career that had done me so much good.

I started to get nervous after the first round was over. I knew there wasn't any chance I'd get drafted that high, but the problem was simple math: only one offensive tackle had been taken, and only one other offensive lineman, Nick Mangold. I figured I'd be somewhere between the seventh and tenth tackle off the board.

Several picks into the second round and still no more tackles had been selected. I really started sweating, got off the couch, grabbed a napkin, dabbed my forehead, started pacing. I must have looked like a mess.

Fuck, this isn't happening right now.

Panic set in. All of these people were sitting quietly around me, the high energy of the start of the draft having faded. Some of them, who didn't quite understand how this all worked, figured I'd be one of the first players off the board. They didn't understand the actual problem with what was unfolding before us with the lack of offensive linemen being selected. They just wanted to know why I wasn't already on a plane to Cleveland.

Fuck, why'd I invite all these people?

Then it happened. Tackles started coming off the draft board. I relaxed a little, but it was for naught. When the Jets made the ninety-seventh pick of the draft and it wasn't me, I started doubting everything I had done in my life up to that point. It felt like a complete rejection of all the hard work I had put in. First I thought about all the surgeries I'd had. Did they scare off all these teams? I had crushed it my senior season, and I assumed that would show the entire league I was good to go. Was it not enough? Then I thought about all of these people I had just let down. The vibe at Starr's house was like a rodeo when the bull-rider just got trampled. People didn't know quite what to say. *I* didn't know what to say. The first day of the draft had come and gone, and I was still waiting for a phone call on Starr's couch. My whole football career, everything had always worked out in my favor until that first day of the 2006 NFL Draft. In the end, people drifted quietly out of the house with some soft words of encouragement. I wasn't encouraged.

I wondered if I'd made a mistake hiring Aaron's team ahead of the draft. The same exact thing had happened to him just one year earlier, sliding down the draft well below where people assumed he would be selected. Was Aaron's crew just not up to the task? Sitting with my friends and family next to a silent phone for several hours during the draft was embarrassing, but thinking about Aaron made me grateful that my humiliation wasn't being played out on live national television. Not many people outside of Redding were wondering why I hadn't been selected yet.

I didn't want to see anybody that night, so I booked a room at one of the local hotels. The one person I wanted there was Brian. I knew he and I could shoot the shit all night and not talk about football or what had happened. After we checked into the hotel we ordered some food to be delivered for dinner. I didn't want to leave that room until I had to the next morning, and I certainly didn't want to go to a restaurant in town. I knew I'd run into idiot strangers who would ask me absolutely brilliant questions about not being drafted. So we ordered in and stayed up chatting.

As we sat there lying on our beds talking about everything but football, the same thought kept running through my head: *Does the NFL know I'm gay?*

Were the teams colluding to reject me because I liked guys? Had I not covered all of my tracks? It suddenly dawned on me that all of my assumptions about playing in the NFL one day may have been a house of cards, toppled by my secret that someone in the corner of some NFL office had figured out and shared with the rest of the league. There would be four more rounds of the draft the next day, but my life suddenly felt in the balance like never before. Depression had not been a foreign concept to me, particularly during the off-season. Lying there trying to bury the overwhelming disappointment of the day, crazy thoughts went through my head. I struggled to sleep more than a few winks that night.

The next day, back at my parents' house, only a couple friends came over. I wasn't going to have a repeat of the night before. I really didn't want anyone around in case total disaster struck on day two. Also, my parents' living room had only a couple small couches and not room for more than a handful of people. Starr really wanted to be there, so she joined us. Brian was there too. We had a subdued and super-nervous second-day gathering.

My agent had been on the phone the night before and again that morning assuring me that I'd get drafted. But this was the same guy who thought I'd already be at my new stadium wearing the team's cap and talking to the local media. There were two teams we thought were most interested: the Cincinnati Bengals, who had interviewed me at the NFL Scouting Combine, and the Cleveland Browns, who had been asking questions of my agent. Between the two of them, they had three fourth-round picks. Yet as we sat there that Sunday morning, those picks came and went. Evidently, the two teams most interested weren't interested anymore. The sweat started pouring out of me again. At the end of the fourth round I called my agent, who again assured me I'd get a phone call from somebody. After that I was checking my phone every minute, pacing around the room.

How the fuck is this happening?

When the phone rang, it was from a 508 area code. I couldn't answer it fast enough.

"Ryan, this is Berj Najarian from the New England Patriots. Please hold for Coach Belichick."

I don't really remember what else was said on that phone call. I know head coach Bill Belichick got on the phone, told me they were drafting me, and welcomed me to the team. He probably said something deadpan about competing for a job. By the time the team's owner, Robert Kraft, got on the phone, my mind was spinning as I watched the joy pour out of my family and friends. With Mr. Kraft it was never a quick hello. He seems to genuinely like people. Even that day we chatted for a few minutes, despite him having to get back to business as soon as my pick was made.

There I was, standing in my parents' living room with the sportswriter clicking some photographs, one minute upset that the lowly Browns didn't pick me and the next minute talking to the two men who had built the NFL's latest dynasty as they welcomed me to the team.

Holy shit, I just got drafted by the Patriots.

New England selecting me was a big surprise. I couldn't remember ever speaking to anyone with the team before that phone call. My agent didn't remember any conversation of substance with them either. My parents had been hoping I would end up on the West Coast, as they wanted to continue following me. Instead, the team farthest away from Redding had grabbed me. I was fine with it. No, I was absolutely thrilled about it. The Patriots were the NFL's best team. And their reputation preceded them. With them, everything was focused on doing your job. No egos. No attitudes. No bullshit, just football. And, for me, my secret. I would be moving to the absolute perfect spot. Plus, I knew my dad would get over the distance. Having a son on the Patriots, with a real shot at playing in a Super Bowl, could justify any cross-country trips he might have to make to watch me play.

I wasted no time getting to a computer to size up the roster, see what other tackles I would be competing with for a spot. Just the year before they had used a third-round pick on another offensive tackle, Nick Kaczur. I was just a fifth-round pick, and plenty of fifth-round picks get cut three months later by the very team that drafted them. If I was going to earn a roster spot and get any playing time, I had to be completely prepared when I got to New England.

"Ryan," my mom called from the kitchen, "somebody's here to see you."

When I came into the kitchen, a young boy, the son of one of my dad's officiating buddies, was standing there.

"Oh my god, I can't believe you're a Patriot!" The kid was so excited. He lifted up a Patriots hat for me to sign. His dad was a lifelong Patriots fan, and he had passed that fandom down to his son like my dad had tried so hard to do with me. I talked with the kid a bit, signed his cap, and sent him on his way.

I had certainly experienced some accolades and small-town fame in Redding when I played in high school, and at one point I was literally big man on campus at Cal. That kid running to my house the moment I got drafted, three thousand miles away from the Patriots' Gillette Stadium, was my first real sign that the eyes of an entire nation were on the NFL. Despite the national interest in college football, college football teams are ultimately regional. People in the West watch Cal, Stanford, and USC. People in the Southeast watch Alabama, Florida, and Auburn. Yet the reach of the NFL and its teams, and in particular the New England Patriots, stretches from coast to coast.

Suddenly I felt a bunch of new eyes watching me.

Chapter 5: Welcome to the NFL

"Is it offensive to call you a faggot if you *are* a faggot?"

The ink was barely dry on my rookie contract, and I was sitting in a well-lit conference room in San Diego doing everything I possibly could to disappear. It was the NFL Rookie Symposium, a seminar put on by the league every year. It's supposed to acclimate all the rookies to life in the NFL. You learn about all kinds of stuff, like budgeting and avoiding skanky people just looking for a quick buck. There was also chatter about using drugs, which I'm sure went in and out of the ears of almost every guy sitting in the room. Except for the talk about the testing process. I think each of us was crystal clear about how and when the NFL would be testing us for use of street drugs. I know *I* was.

When I saw that the schedule included a gay former player talking about "homophobia in the NFL," I had a little panic attack right there in the hotel lobby. Football had been my hiding place for almost a decade.

Seeing that topic on the schedule of my first NFL event turned me upside down. It was the first time they'd ever had some gay guy come talk to the players about being gay in the league. In many ways, the NFL really is a reflection of society at large. As some states started to make gay marriage legal, and as athletes were trickling out of the closet, it became an issue the league seemed to suddenly feel the need to talk about. Gay gay gay.

Of all the fucking years to do this, they had to pick my rookie year.

It was meant to help a guy like me, but I didn't want to have anything to do with it. I thought about skipping the session and heading up to my room with a "headache," but there was no way to get out of it. NFL staffers circled the rooms like hawks, and unless I was going to puke on some security guard's shoes, I wasn't going anywhere. If anyone decided to miss a talk or disappeared to their room, they got fined. I didn't need to get fined.

I also knew about that saying, *He doth protest too much.* The guys constantly denying they smoked pot or took pills were probably the biggest addicts on the team. Same thing with the guys who had to throw "faggot" around all the time. I may have dropped that word from time to time, but I knew that if I seemed like I was antigay, that could raise suspicions. If I avoided the gay part of the seminar that day, it might raise some eyebrows that I didn't want raised.

All I kept thinking about as the time for our session with the gay guy approached was how I was supposed to act as if I just didn't care about the topic. What could I do that would tell people I was so uninterested in hearing from a gay guy that I couldn't possibly be gay or antigay? Yeah, all of this shit was going through my head. It always was.

Walking into the room, I stayed as far away from the front of the crowd as possible without looking like I was staying away from the front. I didn't want anyone looking at me, even if it was only the back of my head, while somebody was talking about this shit. I kept my head down, avoided the other players, and sat toward the back. In my fucked-up head, I couldn't sit in the last row. That would have made it look like there was an issue. Hiding was always a game of Goldilocks for me. I had to sit toward the back, but not too far back. It had to be just perfectly far enough away.

Man, this is exhausting.

When the session started and I finally looked up, I got a pit in my stomach. The guy standing at the front of the room wasn't some scrawny little kicker. He wasn't some fit, six-pack-abs cornerback. He was a giant, just like me. Hell, he *was* me. Esera Tuaolo was a defensive lineman for a bunch of teams, playing about ten years including a Super Bowl with the Atlanta Falcons. I'd always felt that the bigger and stronger I got, the easier I could keep my cover. Esera didn't fit one single stereotype I had ever carried about what a gay guy looked like. In our introduction to the league, the NFL was putting this six-foot-two, 280-pound lineman in front of all of us and saying, *He's gay!* Not only that, but he played in the Pac-10 and, oh, he won the Morris Trophy too, just like I did. In my own fucked-up head, all of that put a new target on my back.

How the hell do I get out of here?

For the next half hour my ears jumped between Esera and the voices in my head. They were screaming about how I was supposed to sit in my chair, look up, look around the room, laugh, roll my eyes. What was I supposed to do to look as straight as possible as this gay guy filled the room with gayness?

He talked about living a lie in football and having a boyfriend while he was playing in the Super Bowl. As I sat in my seat listening to him, I was paranoid he would ask me a question. With every word it felt like he was staring right at me.

Then he dropped the bomb.

"I wasn't the only one," he said. "There are other gay players in the NFL."

I literally cringed, trying to shrink my six-foot-six frame into that tiny little seat. It was like Esera was talking about me, like he was pointing straight at me, telling everybody to look at me, and they all knew it. I know he was there to help guys like me, but all I could think about in that moment was how to end this nightmare as fast as possible. When he was done with his talk he dragged it out even more by asking for questions. That's when one guy toward the front raised his hand.

"Is it offensive to call you a faggot if you *are* a faggot?"

Shoot me now.

I'm sure the guy thought he was being funny, and that he'd get a chorus of chuckles from around the room. I sure thought he would. We all knew how homophobic football players supposedly were. We'd all called some gay guy a faggot once or twice, just to prove how manly we were. Yet rather than a bunch of laughs from the guys, I got my first glimpse of what kind of place the NFL really was for a gay guy. There were no chuckles, no smirks. Instead, I saw some heads shaking back and forth. One guy near me muttered under his breath, "Idiot."

Esera handled it like a pro: "Anytime you use it negatively, it's just not right."

The conversation seemed to evaporate into thin air as we filed out of the room, headed to the next session with some former player talking to us about keeping our money in our pockets. I didn't hear a word from any of the guys about what Esera had talked about the entire time we were in San Diego, and I've never heard about it since. Not that I would have. Guys in the NFL just didn't care to talk about gay shit, including the guy at the Rookie Symposium.

I had gotten through it unscathed, but it was a clear signal to me that the NFL was starting to make the presence of gay men in the league an issue to be discussed, whether we wanted to discuss it or not. And if the league was pushing this idea that there are gays in the NFL, it took away some of the luster of the best hiding place I could think of. It was even more important now to do whatever I had to do to look straight and act straight and talk straight.

Truth is, the league's message with Esera missed the mark a bit. Hearing "fag" in the locker room wasn't what made me feel like an outcast in my own sport. That kind of language wasn't in any NFL locker room I was ever part of. Outside of that idiot question posed to Esera, I don't think I *ever* heard that word in the NFL, and it wasn't because of some two-day symposium. Guys entering the league were adults. They'd been to college. They were professionals. Using any kind of hate speech just wasn't on their minds, and they all knew "fag" wasn't a compliment.

Instead, what was a daily reminder that I was "different" from the rest of the guys was the constant conversation in the locker room about women. It happened less intensely in the NFL than in college, but it was there and it was pervasive. The assumption that everyone had a girlfriend or wife. The chatter about hot women or what makes them sexy. The boasting about sexual conquests. I heard it every day in the locker room. Every single day. It was great that the league was trying to do something to help a guy like me by inviting Esera to talk about being good to gay people and keeping slurs out of the locker room. But what guys really needed to do, if they wanted to make the locker room feel to me like I could come out to my teammates, was to quiet the constant talk about sex with women. And yet . . . that's not likely to change anytime soon.

In my own fucked-up way, despite the positive message the league was trying to send, hearing from Esera at the time felt like more harm than good.

* * *

Moving from high school to college football had definitely been a jump for me, but I got acclimated to the college game pretty quickly.

The leap from college to the NFL was overwhelming.

Sure, the move from California to the Boston area had its challenges. Thankfully, I had Brian along with me. He took on essentially being my part-time assistant for a while. He helped find a place for us to live, got the utilities set up, bought furniture, helped move a bunch of shit from Redding. The NFL had warned us at the Rookie Symposium to watch who we surrounded ourselves with, so I was super thankful to have my buddy Brian back in my life again. I couldn't have made the physical move without him. We set up shop in an apartment right near Gillette Stadium, in a town called Walpole that was best known for housing a maximum-security prison. While it might have been nice to live in Boston, keeping the city scene at arm's length, and living down the street from the stadium, was the right move.

The biggest challenge was what took place on the field. It's tough to convey to people in words the difference between major college football and the NFL. One is like a 1999 Toyota Corolla. The other is a 2019 Porsche 911 complete with GPS, Wi-Fi, and Siri.

Everything about the football aspect of the upgrade was a culture shock. The playbook. The studying. The drills. The guys are faster, stronger, and, yeah, smarter. In high school, and even in college to some extent, I could get away with just my size and general athleticism. It was very clear the first day of training camp that July that, to make it in the NFL, I'd need to bust my fat ass constantly. Speaking of which, they needed me to lose more weight. I was already down from my 370-pound high at

Cal, but they wanted me to come in on the scales a lot closer to 330. I could still be the big, sloppy straight guy, I just had to have a little less of the fat.

Making matters simultaneously better and much, much worse, the Patriots needed me right away. The tackle they had drafted a year ahead of me, Nick Kaczur, was dealing with an injury and they were looking for their starter for the first couple months. If I could get up to speed quick enough, not only would I make the team, I'd start week one.

Thank god for Scar. Dante Scarnecchia was the meanest motherfucker I'd ever met in football. Scar was the offensive line coach with the Patriots when I got there. He'd helped keep Tom Brady upright through their Super Bowl runs, and he'd have the gig for a hundred years if he could keep that going. One practice at training camp that year he was playing the role of Brady, taking snaps from center. When one of the snaps jammed his finger, he let out a torrent of screams and chased the center around the field, finally chucking the ball into his player's back. If you crossed Scar, whether you meant to or not, you were going to pay for it. He was totally nuts.

He was also the best coach I ever had. He genuinely cared about his players. He was interested in us as people, in our personal lives, and in what made us tick. He had a house in Narragansett on the coast of Rhode Island, and he'd invite the linemen there just to spend time with him and his wife and build a deeper relationship. I actually felt a sense of loss by not being able to share who I really was with Scar. Looking back at it now, I probably could have. At the time, there was zero chance in hell I'd do that.

On the field there was no one better than Scar at teaching the game. He had a way of tearing you down just to the breaking point, and then helping you build yourself back up again.

He knew how to instruct people, and how to motivate them. He truly cared not just about the team, and not just about winning, but about each of his players as individuals. He wanted us to succeed as both players *and* people. Even if he could be a fucking asshole.

There's no way I would have started week one my rookie season without Scar, but there I was at Gillette Stadium in early September 2006, wearing number 68 and blocking for Tom Brady and Corey Dillon. The Buffalo Bills were in town. They had been the Patriots' punching bag since Bill got there. The week leading up to the game we heard all of the usual stuff about not taking anything for granted, focusing on doing our job. But the atmosphere on the team was really confident. Maybe overconfident.

A couple hours before the game, Scar asked me to join him in the O-line meeting room. Just him and me. He put up some film for me to watch showing the Bills' defensive end I was going up against and a tackle—I think from the Baltimore Ravens—who he felt had handled the pressure well. What Scar didn't know is that I had already watched this entire game as part of my extensive film study. Like I said, I made film study a hallmark of my preparation.

"If you get number 12 hurt," he said to me in the moments before the game, "it's your ass." Number 12 was Tom Brady. The franchise quarterback. The future Hall of Famer, arguably the greatest quarterback to ever play the game. Hell, if I got Tom hurt, I'd cut myself. But . . . no pressure.

After the kickoff we took the field for the first offensive play of the game. I had already soaked in the atmosphere of my first NFL game, hitting the field early so my head was focused on the football when it mattered. My parents had come to just about every one of my games at Cal, but I wasn't expecting them to make it to Foxborough, Massachusetts, very often. Getting from Redding to Foxborough was hell. Yet make the trip they did for my first game, so I particularly wanted to put on a good show for them. They knew the drill about keeping distance on game day, and getting a couple tickets for them was as easy as putting my name on a piece of paper. I was able to just focus on the game.

By the time I got into my three-point stance, ready for my first NFL snap, I was prepared. I had studied hard, I had practiced hard, I had made the team and earned a starting spot in week one. Plus, we had carefully scripted what we were going to do that very first play of the game. It would be a pass play to the right side, and I was ready for my assignment.

"HIKE!"

I dropped back into pass coverage and held my ground. It felt good to get one over on the defender on my first NFL snap. No way I was going to let anybody touch number 12 on the first play of the game. Then suddenly, a moaning roar came across the stadium. I spun my head around trying to figure out what was going on. As I looked to my right, I saw the football rolling on the ground.

What the fuck?

One of the Bills, London Fletcher, was running at the ball, and before I could react he was scooping and scoring. I looked behind me and saw that the Bills had wreaked chaos on the line. When I asked one of the guys what happened, he told me that Takeo Spikes had blasted right through our line, sacked Tom Brady from his blind side, and forced a fumble. I'd had my back turned to it all and never had a shot at making the stats sheet with a recovery.

You have to be fucking kidding me.

Part of me was relieved Spikes hadn't come from my side,

and that I hadn't gotten number 12 injured. But I also knew it didn't matter much. The offensive line was a unit, and any of us giving up a sack went on all of us. Let alone a sack-fumble. Returned for a touchdown. Against the Bills. Scar was going to have a field day with this one.

It sucked to be in a touchdown deficit almost before the game had started, but after Scar's personal warning to me, I was frankly just glad Spikes hadn't come through my side.

We went on to win that game by a safety, 19–17. It was my introduction to how the Patriots did things: they just found a way to win. It was also an introduction to the team's right guard, Steve Neal. I was lucky to play next to Steve that first game and almost every other game I played in for the Patriots. He brought so much experience, having played in three Super Bowls by that point. He was smart, he knew all the plays, and he knew all the adjustments. We had been working together in camp—no doubt somebody said, "Make sure the rook is up to speed." So we had some experience together. I knew if something came up that was weird, like in the middle of Tom's cadence, he'd be able to tell me, "Get *that* guy," and it would work out.

When Nick Kaczur was healthy again he went back into the starting lineup. There was an unwritten rule that you didn't lose your starting job to an injury (unless, of course, your name is Drew Bledsoe and you play for the New England Patriots), so I understood why I was backing up Nick by October. At Cal I had started every game for almost three years, so it was strange to be back on the bench. When we lost the first two games Nick started that season, part of me wondered where we would be if I was back with the starters. But I knew Nick was their guy. He'd have to get reinjured for me to start again.

One of the best things for me about being in the NFL was that

I got to ditch my "asshole" act that had plagued me for so many years. Of all the things I did to hide my sexuality in high school and college, being a "brutally honest jerk" was the thing that ate at me the most. It wasn't who I was. In the NFL, trying to pull that shit, I—even at my size—would have gotten my ass kicked.

Also, it just wasn't necessary. My NFL teammates didn't see behind the curtain the way the guys in college had. I wasn't living with any teammates when I got to New England. So there wasn't anyone checking in on a daily basis to see whether or not I was hooking up with women. The time you spend with teammates goes way down when you enter the NFL. Guys are professionals. They have their own lives, their own families, wives, kids. I learned quickly that I could actually be nice to people again, and they responded well to that.

Plus, as soon as I got to Foxborough, my best hopes for the team were realized. The Patriots' reputation of hard work and success were spot-on. All I was there to do in New England was whatever it took to win. Period. Distractions were not allowed. I did sometimes think about what that meant for me as a gay man. I can only imagine what kind of "distraction" it might bring to the team if anyone knew I was gay. Would the team cut me the next day, to get rid of the "distraction"? While I felt more comfortable being on the Patriots than I ever had on any other football team, the team's maniacal avoidance of any distractions did at times weigh on my mind.

Still, the complete focus on doing my job did ultimately help. Being on a team in general kind of helps. You're around these same people all the time, but you're also able to kind of hide on that team. The way the locker room was, people knew each other's personal lives but there seemed to be little cliques on each team. A lot of the focus remained within those groups. I was on the offensive line, so I hung out mostly with the offensive linemen. I didn't have to answer many questions from the running backs or the safeties. They stuck to their groups and I stuck to mine.

Of course, questions about girlfriends came up from time to time. We were there to work, but we weren't robots. You hang out at training camp and in and around the stadium enough and people will start asking about more than sweep plays and fumble recoveries. Luckily, they knew nothing about my past. So I made up a fictitious relationship back home in Redding. The woman was real, but the relationship wasn't. I had known Katie since kindergarten. A truly sweet, wonderful person. She was part of the band and drama crowd I had been friends with. She always seemed to take kindly to me, even after I gravitated away from our friend group toward the athletes. We never had sex or anything, but she was just always around in my life. If I had asked her to marry me in those years, I think I might have had a shot. And our lives together might have been fine. But I just couldn't do that to her. I knew then that it wasn't right to put a woman through that just so everyone else would think I was straight. She deserved more than just a "fine" marriage that would have been completely unsatisfying both in and out of bed.

It wasn't out of the ordinary at all for a guy like me to have a "high school sweetheart," and I quickly found that any questions about why I wasn't hooking up with women or chasing skirts were effectively answered with just a few details about Katie, the "girl back home." Guys on the team didn't know fuck-all about me, so I could create the story I wanted. And nobody ever asked why Katie hadn't moved to New England with me. There were plenty of guys who had girlfriends back home. No questions asked. While we cared for each other on the team and wanted the best for one another, at the end of the day nobody felt the need to know every detail about "the girl in California."

When other guys brought dates to events, Brian was usually my plus-one. It wasn't unusual for a player like me to have a best-friend-slash-assistant hanging out all the time. And Brian knew about Katie. I'd mentioned to him that I could see myself marrying Katie at some point. If guys ever, for some reason, asked Brian about her, he'd have some intel to corroborate my story.

There was one time when I had to get a bit creative. Patriots owner Robert Kraft and his wife Myra were celebrating their forty-fifth wedding anniversary, and all the guys on the team were invited. You just don't bring your buddy as your guest to a wedding anniversary. It's supposed to be a celebration of love, and the last thing I ever wanted was for someone to get the wrong idea about Brian and me and start asking questions.

The Krafts were going all out for the big celebration. They covered much of the field at Gillette Stadium with a giant white tent, and they invited hundreds and hundreds of people. Elton John, whom I would later learn was a personal friend of Mr. Kraft, gave a private performance for the crowd. The fact that Elton was gay never crossed my mind, he was just a music legend and he transcended all of that. There was five-star catering, and top-shelf liquor on every table and at every bar.

Billionaires sure know how to throw a party.

My date for the evening was the ex-girlfriend of a former college teammate of mine. She was living in New York City, and we had stayed in touch at some level since college. I let her know up front that we would be going as "just friends." I didn't want her to feel uncomfortable, and I didn't want there to be any question about a hook-up following the party. After all, I had my girl back home, who just couldn't seem to make it out to Foxborough for the festivities. I think she thought I was doing her a favor, asking her to come to this tricked-out party at an NFL stadium, but in reality she was saving me that night. Showing up with a cute woman on my arm I knew would continue to keep any thoughts about me being gay away from the team. It worked perfectly. The guys took to her and she fit right into the group. Crisis averted.

The Sunday after Thanksgiving of my rookie season was one of those perfect New England fall days you hear about. The sun shining through passing clouds, light breeze, midfifties. The kind of weather that was made for football. I always liked when it cooled off. My whole life I'd been self-conscious about how much I sweat, even sitting in air-conditioning. Playing in California I was drenched all the time, soaking right through my uniform. The cooler temperatures in New England were a great change of season for a sweaty 300-pounder like me.

A week earlier we had headed to Green Bay to play the Packers. It was my first trip to Lambeau Field, so I was sure to be on the first bus to the stadium. I always went out early to the field. It was part of my routine—to get acclimated to the place, get my mind into the space. I also wanted to see Aaron, who had been drafted to back up Brett Favre. I grabbed some chew from my locker and headed to the field ahead of almost everyone else, settling onto a bench on our side of the field.

"Welcome to Lambeau, Tool," Aaron said as he walked toward me. "Tool" was his pretty unoriginal nickname for me, drawn from the sometimes dopey, backward comments I'd make in college.

"It'll do for the day, Bubs." That was my nickname for him, short for "Bubbles." It came from this joke I used to hear. You'd ask someone if they blew bubbles when they were a kid. When they said yes, you'd say, "Oh, I talked to Bubbles yesterday and he told me to say hi." Me cracking a gay joke and nicknaming my friend after it.

I am fucked up.

"Did you ever think back in high school that we'd be standing here together?" Aaron asked.

"Hopefully this one ends the same way it did in high school," I replied. It did. After two losses before that game, we steamrolled the Packers. By the time Aaron came into the game it had already been decided. Our defense blanked the Packers, and we poured thirty-five points on them. There wasn't much Aaron could do.

When the Bears came to Gillette Stadium a week later, it felt like a possible preview of the Super Bowl. They were 9-1 and their defense was playing really well, in large part because Brian Urlacher was shutting down everything that came his way. Everybody knew it was going to be a low-scoring, defensive struggle, which put a lot more pressure on the line to keep Brady upright and keep the train moving down the field. Finding success against that Bears defense would be tough, so when opportunities opened up we'd need to take every single one.

It was a late-afternoon start, which was perfect. The sun was setting, the cooler temperatures were rolling in. Just how I liked it. My parents even made the cross-country trip to be there for the game. They hadn't been there since the opening game of the season, and it was great to have them around. That morning before the game, they kept their distance as always, but we would be sure to connect that night.

The game was a battle from the opening kickoff. It was the fourth straight week we went up against a playoff-bound team, a brutal midseason stretch, and everybody knew the postseason was at stake that night. It was still scoreless early in the second quarter, and quarterback Rex Grossman had the Bears driving.

I hadn't started the game, but I was going to go in on the next series, so I was busy with Scar and the guys talking about the next drive. We linemen were never standing on the sideline watching the action. Us big fat guys wanted to get off our feet whenever we could. Plus, we had a lot of work to do between series, looking at photos of the defensive schemes, talking about what trends we were noticing, listening to Tom share what he'd seen. I kept peeking up to see where the Bears offense was on the field, and from my vantage it looked like they couldn't have been more than a few yards away from pay dirt, which meant they'd get on the scoreboard first. Our next drive would be that much more important.

Then, like a cannon, the crowd exploded. Everybody jumped out of their seats to see what was going on.

"Turnover! Turnover!" a couple guys were screaming. The defense had done it again.

I slammed on my helmet and came onto the field. Walking into a Tom Brady huddle wasn't the most intimidating experience. Tom was pretty routine in the huddle. As long as you knew the playbook—and I knew the playbook—you were fine. His instructions always came the same way. Formation, then play, then snap count. Tom had learned at least one thing from Bill: if you kept it routine, it became routine. So his instructions in the huddle weren't anything spectacular. It was after the huddle that the fireworks started.

Tom would usually wait to watch the defense, then he'd call out the mike linebacker—the middle linebacker—on each play. Sometimes he would call out a safety who had dropped down. What he was trying to do was arrange the blocking scheme in a way that would benefit the play that was called. Depending on where he needed protection or the running back needed space, he would arrange the offensive line's blocking according to the defensive player he felt was in the "middle" of our set blocking scheme. He'd generally do this three to four seconds before the snap, sometimes changing it all with even less time to adjust. That first season, with all the starts I got, I relied on Steve Neal a lot more to help me figure out who my key was as the snap was imminent.

A crucial play of the drive was going to be a Laurence Maroney run coming my way. It was a beautiful thing. I listened for the posthuddle instruction, jumped on the snap, sealed the edge, and one of the guys pulled from behind to get an extra block. Maroney went for seven yards, and the coaches put a big, bright mental asterisk on that one.

A few plays later we were still on the field, and we were well inside field goal range facing a second and short. The call came in to Tom: we'd run that same play with Maroney but reverse it. This time I'd be pulling left. As we got to the line, Tom called out the middle linebacker. It was Urlacher. The play required me to haul ass behind the line and block Urlacher, clearing the way for the running back to get into the secondary. In my ten years playing football I'd run that play a thousand times.

At the snap, I cut behind the center ready to lead the way for—

POP!

I was down.

Out. Cold.

Gone.

When I came to, I was surrounded by a few teammates just getting off the turf. I couldn't have been out for more than a few seconds. As I lay there, a couple guys started jabbering at me, trying to get my attention, but all I could think about in those first several moments was my overwhelming awareness of one thing.

"I can't feel my legs."

Everybody jumped back away from me like I was a bomb. All hell broke loose. Guys started screaming, whistles started blowing.

"Ryan, just don't move," Matt Light said.

I can't.

I couldn't move my hands, either.

Fuck!

The training staff was suddenly on top of me. More "don't move" and a series of questions. Everything got really serious, though I couldn't hear much over the voices in my head.

Paralyzed.

That's what kept going through my head.

I'm paralyzed.

My NFL career would be over right as it got started. I wasn't just going to be a faggot, I was going to be a paralyzed faggot. In a wheelchair, somebody having to feed me. Oh, fuck no. I couldn't have that. Gay and paralyzed?

Oh god, please make my legs move.

"Bring out the cart!" somebody said into their radio.

Fuck, I am not being rolled off this field.

My body was twitching a little, like trying to jump-start an engine.

Then a blast of heat raced through my body. Never felt anything like it before or since. The engine jump-started and suddenly I could wiggle my toes again. I could feel my fingers, the weirdest tingling sensation like rubbing grains of sand between my fingers as hard as I could. It was strange, almost painful. But I could move again.

Oh fuck, thank god.

I sat up with people screaming at me to lie down, but I was way too stubborn for that. Us big guys on the line, the whole macho thing isn't just an image, it becomes a way of life, even for a guy like me. No way in hell I was going to let myself be carted away if I could help it. By then I was getting to my feet. I couldn't quite feel those feet, but I could feel the pressure of 330 pounds on them. With a guy under each arm, I stood up and hobbled off the field. People always applaud when an injured player leaves the field. It might seem like just a courtesy sitting in the stands, but man, it feels good to hear.

Coach Belichick had come onto the field. For a guy always thinking about the next play, it was nice to see him show that he cared. Even though I'd started a bunch of games already, I was still a rookie. It meant a lot to see him off the sideline and coming out to check up on me.

As soon as I walked into the locker room and sat on a table, a trainer cut my jersey right off of me. Didn't want to risk anything, even with me putting my arms over my head and pulling the shirt off my back. The team didn't have all of the machines to do the tests I needed, so they put a neck brace on me and another trainer drove me to Massachusetts General Hospital in Boston, about an hour north. My neck was stiffening up by then and really starting to hurt. As we drove to the hospital I could feel my hands and feet a little better. Whatever pain was headed my way, I was just thankful to be walking around.

I was at the hospital into the early hours of the morning. Between just about every spine and neck test known to humans, I was busy texting my parents and Brian. My mom, of course, was a wreck about it. No parent takes seeing their son flat on his back with an injury very well. Of all the games for them to come watch. I was glad to have Brian there with them to calm them down and get them what they needed while they waited for updates. Ultimately, all of the tests checked out and they sent me home in a neck brace. My season had gone so well until then, and the team was rolling. Now the team was telling me to just stay home on Monday and rest.

By Wednesday it was back to the grind. I knew I wouldn't be playing that Sunday, and probably not for a while. Lifting and any physical training were out of the question until I was cleared. Even the physical therapists took it easy on me that first week. No one wants to fuck around with a neck injury. And by now my neck was killing me. I was using some Vicodin to cut down on the pain, but the regular-sized doses I was taking just weren't going to stop the knife in the side of my neck from twisting until my shoulders and upper back started to get tight too. Taking a bunch of time away from the film study and position meetings because of some neck pain just wasn't an option. With the Patriots, if you're not keeping up, you're getting left behind. I had grown very quickly to love the Patriots culture that had a way of burying so much of my life in the recesses of my mind and putting football front-and-center. I didn't mind hitting the classrooms and film review. By midseason I'd found a home with these guys. I wanted to be around them.

Every week Scar put together a video of plays that failed and plays that were successful. As we were watching the film one afternoon, my blackout play came up and I finally got to see what happened. It seems the Patriots coaches hadn't been the only guys who made a mental asterisk about that first successful Maroney run. Like any of the great middle linebackers, Urlacher was a coach on the field. The guy was a fucking genius. That play was vintage Urlacher. He read it perfectly, got to the edge of the line in a flash, and, before I even saw him coming, earholed me, driving my head sideways, and slammed me to the ground.

Man, he was good.

Scar had put that play on the list of successes. While it

might have ended my season, Maroney ran for eight yards behind me absorbing Urlacher's crushing blow.

"You can't put that play on this list," Steven Neal piped up.

Scar asked him why not.

"Come on, man. Ryan got knocked out."

Scar peered up at the screen, then looked over at Steven like
he was speaking another language. He was.

"But we gained eight yards," Scar said.

I wasn't mad at him. That was just the Patriot way. The play
did work. On the field it was a success, and most importantly,
we won the game. "O'Callaghan Left" still had some juice in it,
even if it came damn near to ending my season.

A few weeks later I did come back. I was on the field again
in week seventeen before they shut me down for the playoffs.
That game was uneventful for me, except I did learn a valuable
lesson. While they were paying me hundreds of thousands of
dollars that season, when I came back in week seventeen, the
jersey they had cut off of me a few weeks earlier was hanging
in my locker. It wasn't a souvenir, I'd be wearing it in the game.
They had sewn the jersey back up for a few bucks, instead of
spending two hundred dollars on another *O'Callaghan 68* jersey. This wasn't about salary caps or any other rule they had to
live by. The NFL and its teams counted pennies, and they didn't
let any of those pennies walk out the door unnecessarily. It's a
league-wide philosophy that would cost me dearly long after
my retirement.

 **Chapter 6: The Losers' Ring**

I recovered and played the entire 2007 season as Nick's backup. There was one game that season, though, when he was injured and I stepped into his place. That one start during our near-perfect 2007 season happened to be the biggest game of my career, and one of the biggest NFL games in decades. It was the last game of the regular season, and we were playing the New York Giants in their stadium, trying to complete the NFL's first perfect 16–0 regular season. NBC was broadcasting the game in prime time Saturday night to thirty-five million viewers. None of that mattered to me. With all the external commotion swirling about our team record, it was business as usual in Foxborough and I had a job to do.

There was a sign on the door as you entered the facility that season that either hadn't been there before, or I simply hadn't noticed. I don't remember exactly what it said, but it was something like, *Do your job. Ignore the noise. Put the team first.* It was essentially Bill's standard rules of shut up, ignore everyone, and do your job. The reminder was important. That season had started out rocky. We dismantled the New York Jets in the first week, but our former defensive coordinator, Eric Mangini, who was the Jets' new head coach, had decided to raise hell by accusing Bill of illegally videotaping a bunch of shit from other teams. I don't know about any of that stuff, but I can tell you that I never saw videos of other teams practicing or their signals or anything else. What I did know is that we were so incredibly prepared every week to go up against our opponent that, frankly, I doubt some recording of the other team would have mattered one bit.

I bring that up because *Ignore the noise* was a mantra for the team that season. Even as the controversy about possibly recording other teams was rolling through the NFL media, we were simply building toward an undefeated season. Bill never directly addressed it with the team. The closest he came was asking players to repeat the posted *Ignore the noise* edict in team meetings. What's crazy is that it worked. While fans and the media were losing their minds over a possible 16-0 regular season, I almost never heard the players mention it—in the facility, at dinner, or anywhere else. Truly. The guys all believed in Bill 100 percent, and if he told us to ignore the noise, we ignored the noise. We all just kept focusing on the next game ahead.

But of course I wasn't deaf or blind, so I saw the chatter on *SportsCenter* when Brian put it on at the house. Other than that and a few reporters' questions, it just didn't enter my mind. It really didn't. Remember, I just didn't care very much about football or its history. So an undefeated season was neat to be part of, but it wasn't this holy grail that it seemed to be to other people outside the team.

The day after Christmas we were at Gillette Stadium working on the game, the holiday a distant memory. Playing on a Saturday night made for a short week for a team that prided itself on its preparation. Walking the halls was like an ordinary game in September. Particularly in the film room with the offensive line, it was just "next man up." The entire right side of the line would be missing its starters. Nick and Steve were out, which meant that right guard Russ Hochstein and I should be in the film room more than anyone else on the team. And we were. And Kyle Brady, our blocking tight end, was probably out. For the guys in the trenches, we knew it would be an incredible struggle, but we were well prepared for this. Next man up.

I was nervous as hell. I never once vomited from nerves, but there was a swarm of butterflies in my stomach off and on during the week. The thing about Nick being out wasn't necessarily that the starting job fell onto me, but honestly, after me, there wasn't another starting-caliber guy who could step right into that tackle position. If I struggled, there really wasn't anywhere else for the coaching staff to go. Everyone on the line projected a lot of confidence, but inside I knew the team was counting on me in a big way to stay healthy for four quarters. The Patriots practices were no joke. When you were at practice or a film session, you were working your body, your mind, or both. I would leave the facility physically and mentally exhausted. That kept me distracted from the task ahead.

Watching the film that week really helped. I would be facing one of the greatest sack masters in NFL history: Michael Strahan. He was sacking Troy Aikman when I was in sixth grade. I would be going up against someone who wasn't just technically sound, but there was nothing we could throw at him that he hadn't seen dozens of times before. But I had something on my side: the Patriots' film study. Very early on in that week I knew what to expect from Strahan. He wasn't a speed rusher, so he wasn't going to have a lot of success against me on the outside. He'd try to get inside me with a club or a swim move. That would be his play. If I could keep him outside and cut off his inside moves, I'd have a decent day. I was a good matchup for him on our side. Football is a game of matchups, and my footwork was designed to keep a guy like Strahan away from the quarterback. Going into the game, I felt I had a legit chance of getting the best of him. I just had to stick to what I learned from the film study and execute it on Saturday. The other guys in the trenches voiced only 100 percent confidence in me to get the job done.

Out on the practice field with the full team, the vibe was a little different. We had confidence in one another, no doubt, but I was still one of the "backups" starting in one of the biggest regular-season games any of us had ever been in.

"How you feeling?" Randy Moss, our star wide receiver, asked me coming out of a huddle on the field. Randy always got a bad rap from the media and sometimes the public. Totally undeserved. I played with him for two seasons, and the guy was a solid teammate. He was blessed with some of the most amazing talent I've ever witnessed on a football field, but it was his hard work that earned him the success he had. He was always working, always bringing this great, infectious energy to the field. Of course, he rarely talked to the big fat offensive tackle. I knew what was on his mind.

"Feeling good," I said. It wasn't a lie. Because I hadn't started that season, I was in probably the best physical shape of my career. I wasn't battered or even bruised.

We walked through a play and Randy came jogging back to the huddle.

"Strahan's a big boy!" he hollered at me. These moments of needling were his way of testing me, preparing me.

"Randy, I'm bigger." I wasn't into much chatter with my stomach turning itself inside out, but I couldn't resist. Like I said, his energy was infectious. "I'm a little worried about you, though."

He looked at me funny, smiled that smile. He liked the banter, me jabbing him a bit. He was a trash talker, even with his teammates. "Enjoy the show."

* * *

My nerves calmed a bit after our second play of the game. We were already down by a touchdown when we took the field. The weather gods had smiled on us that night—light breeze, low forties. Perfect. According to the media, the Giants didn't have much to play for. They were already in the playoffs and couldn't earn a bye even with a win. But somebody forgot to tell the guys on the team. From the first kickoff it was obvious they were playing to destroy our record. Giants fans, and the players, made it perfectly clear they wanted a win. This game was going to be their own Super Bowl.

Our first play was a quick hit to Randy. First down. I'd gotten my hands on Strahan, but he didn't do much that play, surveying the backfield and seemingly content just taking up space, watching, testing. The one thing I hadn't really gotten a grasp of on the film was the length of his arms. His swim move was a trademark because of those arms. As a lineman you have to keep a guy in front of your numbers to beat him. After that first play, I knew I'd have to contend with those long arms. The second play was the test. Strahan was lined up well outside my right shoulder, head-up on our tight end Ben Watson. At the snap, Strahan came for me on the outside as Tom dropped back behind me. A couple yards into his rush Strahan stuttered—maybe to get inside me, maybe to take a peek at Tom—and I was right there to cut him off. He kept charging on the outside, but he didn't gain a foot. We got another first down on that play with a toss to our other star receiver, Wes Welker.

Fuck, that felt good.

Yet by our third drive I was sucking wind. I had spent the entire season backing up Nick, so I'd seen very little playing time. You can practice till you puke, but there really isn't any way of getting you into game shape other than playing in real games. Even in New England, practices were tough but games were always a whole other level. Whenever our defense was on the field I was on the sideline on the bench, grabbing an oxygen tank. I knew I'd get my second wind eventually, I just had to ride this out.

The rest of the game I held my own. On our first touchdown, Strahan made a really nice move on me to the outside and got right in Tom's face, but Tom had already thrown a jump ball to Randy, so it didn't cost us anything. Halfway through the third, when we were down twelve points, I got a case of the yips. Strahan made a few great moves on me and got right up on Tom just as he tossed the ball into the end zone. A couple of flags negated the play in our favor, but it was a wake-up call. Strahan was elevating his play as the game got tighter in the second half. If I didn't match him, it was going to be a long film review with Scar.

After the flags, the next play was a Maroney run, and I got as low as I could and pushed my way into the end zone. Maroney was right behind me.

On the last score of the game, a Tom-to-Randy touchdown pass that set a couple of NFL records for those guys, it was another play where the line played its ass off. The defense brought five guys. Just as Tom was winding up, I had my hands on two defenders and bought him just enough time. When I looked up and saw the ball coming down, I knew we'd hit pay dirt.

16–0.

We had become the first NFL team to complete an undefeated sixteen-game regular season. I wasn't really in awe of the history of it, but as we celebrated on the field that night it felt like my team and I had accomplished something substantial, something real. We knew we still had two playoff games and a Super Bowl to go win, but that season had been the most draining of my life despite sitting on the bench for most of it. Being able to play every offensive snap for that one seminal victory meant a lot to me. I wasn't just a backup along for the ride. I helped win the big game.

Walking around the field right after the last play, before the place was mobbed, Strahan tracked me down. "Nice job," he said. Maybe it was just typical postgame niceties, but I like to think he meant it. That Saturday night in Giants Stadium, I played the best game of my football career. Not many people can say they got the best of Michael Strahan, but I feel like I'm one of the few. No doubt he got me a couple times. You can't stop a guy like him every play. But I felt great after that game. I felt like I was ready to contribute deep into the playoffs. I felt like we were going to go win the Super Bowl.

With a week off before our first playoff game, and New Year's Eve around the corner, it was time to celebrate a little. A bunch of us headed to Mohegan Sun, a casino in Connecticut, to ring in the New Year together. Most of the offensive line was there. Welker and linebacker Mike Vrabel joined us. While a few of the guys brought their wives or girlfriends, my girlfriend in California was MIA. As always. Brian was along for the fun.

That night we let it all out. We were the 16–0 Patriots, so we got the royal treatment. Plus, guys like Welker were laying down some serious coin at the blackjack table. After one hand when he doubled down and lost, Welker turned to the few of us looking over his shoulder and laid the truth of his nine-million-dollar signing bonus on us: "Thank god I'm rich." There were a bunch of amateur fights that night at the casino, but it was a different fight that would eventually make some headlines.

We were all hanging out in one of the clubs. We got a booth

as home base and wandered the place dancing and drinking. We hadn't been there long when I was sitting in the booth on the side of the dance floor and saw Welker move into a gathering crowd engaged in more than a little pushing and shoving. Any time one of us big guys sees a teammate in a possible altercation, we have no choice but to dive right in. This is what straight guys do: they fight. Apparently Matt Light's wife, dancing up a storm, had said she felt uncomfortable with one of the guys around her. When she said he'd touched her, that's when all hell broke loose. One way to end your night badly is to mess around with an offensive lineman's wife in the presence of a dozen of his teammates. That night there were a bunch of us six-foot-six 300-pounders, so the other guys didn't have much of a chance. Welker was the big name with the recognizable face suddenly caught in the middle of it, so Brian grabbed him and got him out of there. The rest of us no-name giants diffused the situation.

It didn't last long. Security was on top of us pretty quick. When they realized we were all Patriots, and Matt explained what had happened with his wife, they sent the other guys packing. We thought for sure there would be a headline the next few days that we'd pay hell for. "Patriots Celebrate Undefeated Season with Incident at Mohegan Sun." When that didn't materialize, we decided we certainly weren't going to stir the pot and talk about it around the facility. We had escaped Mohegan Sun unscathed.

Despite my good game in Giants Stadium, Nick was back in as the starter at right tackle for the playoffs. When we drew the Giants again in the Super Bowl, I wondered if I had a shot to start. We'd beaten this very team just a month earlier with me in the lineup. We'd given up one sack and, while the entire offensive line gets credit and blame for our collective performance, that

sack wasn't anywhere near my responsibility. Hell, even the referee for the game—Mike Carey—had officiated our December
win. But like I said, you don't lose your starting job to an injury
(unless you're Drew Bledsoe).

Despite not starting, my parents came to the Super Bowl in
Phoenix. For my Dad, a lifelong football guy, it was the culmi-
nation of years of proudly watching his son grow into a football
player and a man. I can picture him almost floating as he chatted up everyone whose ear he could grab in the two weeks leading up to the game. My dad and I had a strained relationship at
times, but football brought us together. I was really happy that
he was there to end that season.

Aaron was there too. Most people, myself included, figured
both Aaron and I would have our teams in that Super Bowl that
year. Instead, the Giants had gone into Green Bay and beaten
the Brett Favre–led Packers in an ice bowl. A couple nights before the big game it was just Brian and Aaron at dinner with
me, shooting the shit and calming my nerves with distraction.
Having Aaron there was a big help, actually. He gave me a good
confidence boost and reminded me that I'd been down this road
before, protecting him in bowl games and the Big Game. When
we were together we almost never talked about football. Many
guys in the NFL rarely talk about the game with one another
when they're off the field. That night with Aaron was no different, but his gentle encouragement was perfect. He always knew
what to say.

It was really tough to watch that game from the sidelines as
the Giants sacked Tom five times and seemed to be in our backfield every other play. The Giants used some different schemes
that day, but it was nothing we couldn't adjust to. Other than
a couple of kicks, I didn't get to play a single down. I hadn't
been afraid of Strahan beating me around the outside when I

matched up with him, but twice he got past Nick on the outside and Tom got sacked. Everyone on an offensive line knows you're not going to win the battle of the trenches every play. The guy on the opposite side is going to get you a handful of times. Our job is to limit the number of times we get beaten, limit the impact of it, and make damn sure it doesn't happen at the wrong time. The second time Strahan just blew past Nick, it was third and seven in the third quarter and we were in field goal range. Nick's feet were stuck in cement that play, and Strahan nailed Tom for a sack. It turned a promising field goal attempt into a missed fourth-down pass. Bad timing.

After the game the locker room was a funeral. The team had scored just fourteen points, by far the lowest total of the season. Guys stuck to themselves in front of their lockers. I just wanted to get in and out of there. It was depressing to see these guys I had come to really like mentally beating themselves up.

Back at the hotel I happened to be getting into the elevator at the same time as Tom and his new girlfriend, supermodel Gisele Bündchen. He was nice enough to introduce us, then I shut up and let him ride in peace. He was noticeably affected by the loss. I wasn't. I simply didn't have a very emotional relationship with winning or losing football games. Don't get me wrong, I would have loved to get a Super Bowl ring. That season had felt like the longest year of my life. Being with the Patriots wasn't easy, and it wasn't for everybody. We put untold hours of work into that season. To come away from it with an *AFC Champions* ring—a losers' ring—wasn't the ending I wanted. That ring now sits buried in my sock drawer.

That night in the hotel there was a big celebration of the season. Mr. Kraft always planned a big party at the hotel after the Super Bowl. I trudged down by myself. The party was elaborate. Bartenders, waiters, food, drink, a deejay—this was a party of all NFL parties. Mr. Kraft had to plan it to celebrate the NFL's first 19–0 season, so it was over the top. One of the first guys I ran into was Matt Light. He hadn't had a great game. Two false starts, a number of blown coverages. He met me with a smile.

"Hey, Ryan, have a drink?" It was the same gregarious Matt I'd partied with on New Year's Eve just a few weeks earlier. I nodded.

"Get my man here a Maker's on the rocks," he told the bartender.

I looked around the room and saw a bunch of veterans laughing, smiling. I was surprised by how many of them had decided to, at least for the night, put the worst loss of their career behind them.

Matt turned back to me with the drink. "Hey, I'll get you that bow as soon as we get back," he said. "Thanks again for that."

I had traded him one of my free hotel rooms that weekend for a hunting bow. I didn't really have any use for it, but it kept up appearances. He and I had talked about hunting a few times, and when he offered, I jumped on it. Matt had been really nice to me, so if the trade could help him and his family over Super Bowl weekend, I was all about it.

I was glad to see Matt and the other guys pushing the emotional wreck of that game into the backs of their minds for that night. There was nothing anyone could do about it now. Might as well have some drinks and listen to some music together. It would be the last time many of us saw one another until months later when we had some organized team activities.

A couple days later I was at Gillette Stadium cleaning out my locker when I ran into Scar. The loss had settled into his soul.

There was a pained look on his face, like he was carrying the whole weight of that loss on his own shoulders. That's just the kind of guy he was.

"I'm sorry you didn't play," he told me. It was a nice gesture on his part.

"You had to go with somebody," I said.

He shook his head. "If we'd made a different decision," he said, "I think we would have had a better chance of winning."

I appreciated that. Like I said before, football is a game of matchups, and I felt I was a better matchup for Strahan than Nick was. But hindsight is twenty-twenty. If the coaches had benched Nick—the guy who'd been on the line for seventeen of our first eighteen wins—and I had faltered, that would have been tough for them to explain to Mr. Kraft, the press, the fans, anybody.

What Scar's comment did tell me was that I had the chance to be in the NFL for a long time. Nick had been their guy, but I had shown them that I had a ton of value. No career is built on one game, but the contrast in our performances against the Giants in those "undefeated" games certainly didn't hurt my chances. While fans and the press don't pay much attention to who's in at right tackle, you bet other NFL coaching staffs do. Despite sitting on the bench most of that season, I proved I belonged. If I busted my ass and played my cards right, I could be in a position to keep myself alive and continue playing football for the Patriots for years to come.

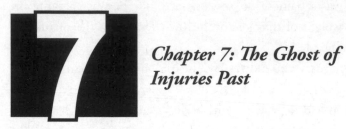

Chapter 7: The Ghost of Injuries Past

After the season ended, I suddenly had way too much time to think. During the season there is so much going on, so many meetings, so many workouts, so much studying. Football consumed my life from July to January. I was often in the film room before anyone else, getting a little extra work in. During that period, there just wasn't any time to feel alone or think much about life. The day after a season ended there was always a huge hole in my life that I was afraid to fill.

It's hard for a lot of people to believe my obsession with looking straight. It consumed so much of my time. Lying and deceiving people had become second nature to me. It had become a part of who I was. Who I *had* to be. And it was during the off-season in the NFL that the worst of my depression set in. At Cal those months were still filled with classes. In the NFL, you need to find your own shit to do when you don't have practices every day. Plus, most of the guys were married, getting married, or had long-term girlfriends. Nobody ever asked, "Why aren't you married?" but when more and more guys around you are tying the knot, there is a subtle pressure to do the same. For now, football was my only beard. When I wasn't going on dates, "I have to focus on football" was a quick excuse. During the off-season that didn't work. I had to come up with something else.

While the Katie excuse worked with the guys on the team, Brian was with me day and night, especially in the off-season. He knew I wasn't going home to see Katie. He knew I went to bed alone every night. And I knew I needed a cover. So every few weeks I'd just disappear for a few hours. I'd make sure Brian was home when I left—usually sitting on the couch playing video games—so he'd see me leave. I always played it exactly like he did when I knew he was going to hook up with some woman. Just grab my keys and silently walk right out the door, all mysterious. I figured if that's what he did, almost like sneaking out of the house, then he'd believe I was doing the same thing.

I'd climb into my pearl-white Cadillac Escalade and head into town. By then we were renting a town house in Bellingham, a couple towns over from Foxborough, from Dan Koppen. It was a postcard of New England. For the next two or three hours I'd just drive around Southeastern Massachusetts. Sometimes I'd stop and get an ice cream cone at the local Friendly's. I always got vanilla. And not that fake vanilla shit, the real vanilla bean. The other stuff—the cookie dough, the hot fudge—just covered the flavor of the actual ice cream, and Friendly's has good ice cream. I'd always stay out of the house long enough for Brian to think that maybe I went and hooked up with a woman, just like he did.

When I got back sometimes he was home, sometimes he wasn't. I never asked him about his excursions, and he never asked me about mine. Brian never gave me any reason to think he suspected I might like guys. Until that summer.

Truth is, I never had sex with anybody those off-seasons, man or woman. While there were ways to find sex with other guys, I never entertained the thought. The possibility of getting "caught" loomed too large for me. Hell, I didn't even look at gay porn. I was scared to death that the wrong person would be at the cash register when I walked out with a magazine, or that Brian would sit down at my computer and stumble across hotgaysex.com in my browsing history. Nothing was worth risking that someone, anyone, might find out who I truly was. I had to keep it all out of sight and out of mind.

One weekend in June, Brian and I headed to the Jersey Shore to hang out with one of my college teammates, Steve Levy, and some other friends for a few days. One of Steve's friends had this gorgeous house on Long Beach Island right on the ocean, the perfect summer weekend escape. That Saturday he had a bunch of guys and girls over to the house. We barbecued, drank, listened to music, drank. As people were crashing well past midnight, Brian and I were still wired, nowhere near time to go to sleep. It was just him and me sitting on the porch sipping on some beer when he asked me.

"Are you gay?"

Brian and I talked all the time. There was always something for us to chew on, whether it was some business venture we wanted to start, a political issue, or gossip about friends. Yet in all the years of knowing him, that question had never come out of his mouth. Nothing even close. So on the one hand, it was pretty out-of-left-field. But I also knew that Brian saw behind the curtain of my life. On that summer night on the Jersey Shore, he let me know he'd started to wonder.

I gave him a disgusted "What?" in return.

"There were a lot of girls here today," he said. "You didn't seem interested in a single one of them."

I'd stayed up a thousand nights rehearsing for when someone asked if I was gay. Every night when I couldn't sleep, this is what I was preparing for.

Like I'd done it a million times, I looked him straight in the eyes. "I'm a lot of things, but gay ain't one of 'em."

That seemed to do the trick. We changed the topic and kept on solving the world's problems even after everyone else had checked out. It's what I loved about my friendship with Brian—we were so often just totally content hanging out with each other and shooting the shit. Yet obviously I had slipped up at some point. He couldn't have just come to that question at one party. He'd been thinking about it. He was such a horndog—nobody took as much interest in women as he did. But he wasn't asking our other buddies if they were gay. He was asking *me*. And I knew I had to run a smarter campaign if I was going to make him forget he'd ever asked that question.

That summer I had my twenty-fifth birthday, so right before the season Brian and I headed back to Redding. The previous season I had gotten a real taste of the "Patriot way," and I knew the season ahead was going to be another arduous Super Bowl run. Escaping New England for a couple weeks to have some semblance of a short summer was important to my sanity.

Brian's parents threw a birthday party for me at their house; they were some of the more well-to-do people in Redding. I guess that isn't saying much, but they did have a really nice house and a pool. I had friends from high school and a bunch of family come from all over Northern California. Aaron even stopped by to hang for the night. He had just finished the American Century Golf Championship in Tahoe a few days earlier, and then he was visiting his parents in Chico, so he drove the hour-plus up the 5 freeway to celebrate with me.

After I'd seen him at the Super Bowl, he'd been anointed the starting quarterback for the Packers after Brett Favre announced his retirement. Though in the days before my birthday party, rumblings were coming from Green Bay that Favre wanted back in. Aaron had stuck around in Chico after the tournament to stay the hell away from the brewing tempest in Green Bay with Favre. My friends and family knew from me that most guys who played in the NFL didn't want to talk about football when they didn't have to, and they respected that with Aaron despite ESPN's sudden wall-to-wall coverage. He knew that by coming to visit me in Redding, he wouldn't have to deal with people asking him about what would soon become the biggest story in sports.

Alone that night, though, Aaron opened up to me. It was like we were still a couple of high school kids, him staying in my sister's old room at my parents' house that night. Away from family and friends, the two NFL guys could talk shop, something we rarely did. I felt for him. He'd been waiting for a few years for his chance to take the reins of an NFL team. But he was really confident in his ability to lead the Packers back to the promised land. Having known him for all those years, and playing with him for a couple, I had zero doubt he could win it all. The whole Favre thing, it really ate at him.

The next day it was just us three guys from NoCal hanging out. Aaron and Brian knew each other from high school, so it was a chill afternoon, no pressures on Aaron from relative strangers. It was a typical scorching-hot day in Redding, so we headed out on my wakeboard boat for the afternoon. We wakeboarded a bunch, trying to put all that waited for us on the football field out of our heads. Two of us with Super Bowls in our minds, it would likely be the last time we'd be able to just let loose for months to come.

The sun was baking us on the turf in Gillette Stadium that July when I finally understood the business of the NFL. I wasn't worried about making the team at that point. I knew I had played well the season before, and the Patriots hadn't drafted a lineman that off-season. Between Nick and me, we had that right tackle spot locked up. Instead of focusing on making the team, I wanted to take Nick's starting spot. Starting right tackles make a lot more money than backups. Plus, this would be the final season in my rookie contract. If I could get some starts, that would mean a heck of a lot in any new contract negotiations.

We were getting some good hits in on the field in nine-on-seven drills. We were working on our running game, which had really struggled in our two games against the Giants the season before. Ty Warren, our stud defensive tackle, was lined up on my inside for a few plays. Ty was an All-Pro in 2007, and he posed a tough matchup for Nick and me. If I wanted Nick's spot, these were my moments to shine.

We broke the huddle for a sweep play and I got into my three-point stance. In the sweep, my job is to freeze that defensive tackle so other guys on the line can get behind me and block the linebackers downfield. When the ball was snapped, I rose out of my stance and met Ty's blazing-fast hands. When you're both three hundred pounds, so much of your effectiveness depends on your hands and feet. On that play Ty got my left wrist and bent it back behind my head. I fell backward, crumpling to the ground as knives dug into my left shoulder.

"Aaaaarrrrgghhh!" I let out a scream that stopped the whole practice. Lying on the ground, I tried to lift my left arm up but *Eek!* It hurt. Even before Ty had wrenched my shoulder, it was already difficult for me to lift my hands over my head after all of my previous college shoulder injuries and surgeries. Luckily, linemen weren't even allowed to catch a football, because there's no chance I could catch a pass above my shoulders.

Fuck! Not again.

Within seconds, two trainers were on the field walking me to the sideline. It was déjà vu all over again. And not from the Urlacher hit. The Patriots had drafted me knowing I'd had three surgeries on my left shoulder in college. All of the surgeries weighed on my draft prospects and had sunk me to the fifth round. I was afraid I'd be paying for it again.

In the training room, Dr. Tom Gill put my arm and shoulder through the motions. He was the head doc with the Patriots. I'd chatted with him a slew of times since getting to Foxborough. Tall guy, balding, seemed thoughtful and bright. I guess that goes without saying.

"It doesn't seem too bad," Doc said, settling my arm by my side. "We can get you some painkillers."

Ummmmmmm, my arm feels like it's going to fall off.

"We're gonna get an MRI, yeah?" I asked.

We did. They scheduled a normal MRI at the facility right away. There was no way in hell my shoulder didn't "seem too bad." I knew shoulder injuries. This was the worst pain I'd ever felt in a shoulder. All of the doctors were out on the practice field with the team, so I slipped into street clothes and waited for one of them to come tell me what the MRI said. I figured it would be Dr. Gill sitting down with me, but he was nowhere to be found. Instead another guy came by with a folder in hand and introduced himself.

"Hi Ryan, I'm Dr. Death." I know that's not what his name was, but frankly, that's what he was to me. "Let's step inside."

He led me to a small, private office just to the side of the training room. I knew it well. That's where they kept the good stuff. If you were in pain in the middle of a game and needed a fix, they took you to that room and closed the door. All the magic potions were in the lower drawer. I'd visited that room more than once. It also felt like an inquisition room. There was a small table, a couple chairs, a little light to view X-rays, no windows. It may have been the most secluded spot in the whole stadium. I sat down on one chair. Dr. Death kept the MRI results clenched in his hand.

"The results are back," he said, "and I'm happy to tell you that nothing new is wrong with your left shoulder."

I can only imagine what my expression was when he said that. He may as well have said, *The Browns will win the Super Bowl this year by defeating the Lions.* After all of the shoulder injuries I'd had, and the knives still sticking in my shoulder since Ty's move, what he was saying was literally impossible.

Fuck you.

"I can't even lift my arm to my chest," I protested.

"We can certainly help with the pain," he said. "But there's nothing new that's wrong with the shoulder." And then the words that really got my head scratching: "You're free to return to practice."

The NFL has an entire protocol in dealing with injured players. As long as you're injured by team activity, you can't be cut. But once you step back onto the practice field, you're not protected anymore and the team can cut you that day if they want to. The Patriots coaches and staff were trying to get me to practice. Why? Because as long as you're injured and unable to play, they have to pay you. The last thing a team wants is a player draining their bank account but not performing on the field. Suddenly I felt like I was in a court case. Anything I said or did could be used against me. I wanted to take a look at the MRI results myself, but I wondered if that would somehow legally make me responsible for understanding them.

I stood up, totally bewildered. Even moving my shoulder to stand up from the chair shot the pain to a nine out of ten. I couldn't lift my arm. I swear it hurt to *think* about lifting my arm. I walked into the locker room, and a few of the guys were still finishing up from practice, including Mike Vrabel. In addition to being one of my favorite people with the Patriots, Vrabel was also our union rep at the time. Every team had one. Every team needed one. I gave him the skinny on my day and told him I suddenly didn't trust the doctors there.

"It's your right to seek and receive a second opinion," he told me.

I barely heard him. "Mike, are they trying to cut me?" It seemed unreal. I was a guy who'd helped them get to 16–0 just seven months earlier. I had proven myself over and over on the field. And I was still young. I had years of NFL playing ahead of me. Was the team that brought me to the NFL now trying to ship me out? I wonder what they would have done if they'd known what I had in store for myself once my career was over. Would they have acted differently?

"They let Asante Samuel go," he said. Asante was a shutdown corner who the Patriots had waved goodbye to a few months earlier. Dr. Death's words kept ringing in my ears: *There's nothing* new *that's wrong with the shoulder.* As though it was some political talking point crafted by Karl Rove. Was he really saying, *Your shoulder is really fucked up again, in all the places your shoulder has been fucked up before?* Some double-speak aimed to get me to practice and cover their asses?

Vrabel reiterated what my rights were as a player and suggested I get another MRI, conducted by someone else, and be sure to see the actual results.

I wanted to use my doctor in the Bay Area, but the Patriots balked. "He's done three surgeries on your shoulder and it's still not right." They actually had a point.

So I got the second MRI done in Boston. This time I controlled the process and made sure it was done right. I asked for an MRI arthrogram, which used dye to help see what was going on in the joint. And I demanded to see the results of the test myself. The radiologist gave me the verdict: dislocated shoulder, torn labrum, partial rotator-cuff tear, torn bicep tendon. I slumped in the chair. So many different emotions raced through me, not the least of which was loneliness. There were guys on the team—like Scar and Matt—who I really felt a great connection to. When I put on that Patriots jersey, I felt real pride to be part of the team. They built an aura around the facility that everyone there was part of something bigger than themselves.

But when my chips were down, and suddenly I might not be worth the few hundred thousand they were paying me, the Patriots had no problem fucking with my livelihood, fucking with my *life*. Their doctor, in that small room with no witnesses and just the two of us sitting there talking, straight-up told me I was good to return to practice. Yet I had multiple injuries to my arm that made it impossible for me to contribute. Impossible. Doctors take an oath to "do no harm." At least one person on the Patriots staff that day turned his back on that oath. In that moment, to them, I wasn't a patient seeking medical advice. I was a business decision.

Fucking assholes.

After that episode I came to believe that the team staff would do absolutely anything to win. I never thought this was just the Patriot way, I always figured it's simply how people do business in the NFL. At least, the people who won on a regular basis. And the Patriots won a lot. You don't win football games with lots of hugs and kisses. You win football games by putting the best product on the field. That singular focus on winning was one of the main reasons I was happy to be in Foxborough. I knew that all the coaches cared about was football. In those moments, though, when I was hurting and feeling completely abandoned, it certainly didn't feel very good.

* * *

That "season," Brian had the idea that I should get a dog. It was genius. We saved Taylor from a boxer puppy mill, where she would have been tortured, used to breed all her life. Instead she got stuck with me. Thank god. I needed someone around the house to keep me going.

Taylor transformed my life. Suddenly I had something else that relied on me to live. Since I wasn't playing, I got to take care of her myself the first year she was with us. I brought her to the vet for her checkups. I learned she had an absolute fascination with tennis balls, whether it was chasing, retrieving, or gnawing on them. I got to know her personality, which showed through when she would toss her entire basket of toys around the room just to find the specific one she just had to play with at that moment. She was also another mouth to feed. Sure, I generally bought the food around the house for Brian and me, but he had his own job, his own ability to take care of himself, most of the time. Taylor was totally reliant on me to take care of her. It was a new concept to me. Since high school all I had to do was show up to class, study the playbook, and get strong and fat. The addition of Taylor felt like the birth of a true purpose for my life.

Recovery from the surgeries was long. As soon as I was well enough to do rehab, I was back at Gillette Stadium working with the staff there. I was resigned to being kicked to the curb by the team after the season, but football was still my lifeline. If there was any chance to make the team next year, I wanted to show them I could do it. Hitting the training facility every day all season, while the team was playing, told them I was committed. They could see my progress firsthand. Of course, with his week-one injury, I saw Tom a lot in the facility that season too.

No matter how shitty rehab went that day, Taylor was always happy to see me. She may have shit on the rug three times, but she'd still be there greeting me at the door, barking and wagging her tail like nothing was wrong. I could yell at her, refuse to throw the tennis ball, and lock her outside in the yard until she took care of her business. She'd just come right back in the house, rub against me, lick my face, and put her head on my lap. I guess they call that love.

Responsibility and love. I never really had those two things until Taylor.

"Have a seat, Ryan." Those were not the words anyone wanted to hear from Bill Belichick. Yet there I was the Saturday after our final preseason game a year later. The legend himself had invited me to a one-on-one conversation. I'd had only brief interactions with him since taking his phone call on draft day three years earlier. He was a defensive guy, and I was an offensive tackle. As long as he wasn't talking to me, it was good news. This meeting was bad news.

I had gotten one start that preseason after my injury. It was, of course, against the Giants. A few months earlier the team had used a second-round pick on Sebastian Vollmer. He was a couple inches taller and a bit more mobile than I was. I knew what the tea leaves read.

"Ryan, I'm in a tough spot here," Bill said. He was never known for bullshitting, so I took him at his word. "There's a player we've been trying to move, and the trade just isn't getting done."

"I understand," I said, sliding my playbook onto his desk.

"We need that roster spot for just a few days. And between now and then, you're probably going to get a phone call from Scott Pioli." Pioli had been with the Patriots when they drafted me, and he was the new general manager of the Kansas City

Chiefs. I hadn't spent much time with him, but I knew him as a bright guy who always had a nice word to say when you passed by him.

"I appreciate that, Coach."

We got up, shook hands, and I was out the door.

Fuck, what am I going to do?

There are never guarantees of a second shot in the NFL, and I started freaking out. Guys got cut all the time, never to be seen on the football field again. And I was an "injury-prone" guy now sitting on the sidelines. I called my agent and gave him the news. He had to find me a spot. Without football, my pact with myself would have to be fulfilled.

It wasn't twenty-four hours before Pioli called me with a lifeline. Not only did he ask me to join him with the Chiefs, but they wanted to slide me right into the starting spot. He'd already brought over a couple other guys from the team—Matt Cassel, the backup QB who had played so well for the Patriots while Tom was with me in rehab, and Mike Vrabel.

I'd always been the fill-in guy in New England behind Nick. Now I would be one of the leaders on my new team. And I'd be making starter money. Plus, although it wasn't the West Coast, it was halfway to being back home. My parents had only made it to a couple games in Foxborough, and I figured playing more regularly and being just a few hours' flight from San Francisco would get them to more games. It seemed like an absolute dream scenario to me.

Chapter 8: Total Shit Show

As soon as I got to Kansas City, I knew we were in big trouble. While the general manager, the quarterback, a defensive leader, and I had all come from the win-or-else Patriots, the head coach . . . hadn't. Todd Haley had been the offensive coordinator with the Arizona Cardinals, who had managed to have a good run in January and get to the Super Bowl. The Cardinals were never truly great when he was there, but he had been the latest guy dubbed an "offensive genius." So he was brought in by the Chiefs to whip a team that had some trouble moving the ball around the field. It was an exciting time with a lot of hope when I got to Kansas City.

By my second week with the team, however, before I even got to play with them, it was clear we were going nowhere.

It was toward the end of one particular practice and the special teams were on the field doing their thing. In New England, while special teams were working on their game, the offensive line was going through drills. There was no downtime. If you were practicing, you were working. That day with the Chiefs, the guys not on special teams went to the bench and sat down. Relaxed. That told me a lot about the culture of the team I'd just landed on. I knew right then that there wouldn't be a single team we played all season that we had outworked during the week.

It was a reflection of Todd. You hear all the time about "players' coaches." He was a players' coach. He wanted to be one of the guys, he wanted to be liked by the athletes on the team. One of the ways he did that was to say "no homo" a lot. He had gotten it from some Jay-Z song he listened to or some shit like that. Haley was listening to rap music all the time, I guess because that's what he thought would make him more likable with some of the guys on the team.

Todd used "no homo" in meetings, at meals, passing him in the hallway. It was fucked up. As a closeted gay dude in the meetings with him, having to hear that over and over and over cemented the already concrete idea in my head that I could never, ever, ever come out to him or the team.

I was always one of the first players to get to the facility each day—it was the Patriot way. One morning I could feel my truck shake from the booming music of somebody's car pulling up behind me. I figured it was one of the DBs blasting Kid Cudi from his Range Rover. When the car slipped into the parking spot beside me, I saw it was Todd, sitting low in his seat like a gangsta, barely able to see out the windshield. He was trying so hard to fit in with the players. It was a 180 from what I'd experienced in New England. I laughed my ass off over that one.

For some reason when we were alone together, which happened from time to time that first season, Todd would insist on bad-mouthing Scott Pioli to me. My guess is that he thought I was a "Pioli guy" because he'd brought me over from New England. From the first weeks with the Chiefs, it was apparent that there was a big rift growing between the GM and the HC. Todd would test me, talking smack about Pioli, seeing if I would defend him. I didn't get any of the shit he was saying; Pioli always seemed like not just a good man, but also pretty bright. I kept my mouth shut for the most part, only adding little comments or nodding enough to acknowledge what Todd was saying in an attempt to stay on his good side. All of the politics and gossip weren't my thing. If you were part of the gossip, the gossip would eventually turn around and focus on you. That was the last thing in the world I could survive.

Do your job. Ignore the noise. Put the team first.

That season was the mess I knew it would be. We went 4–8 when I started, losing the other four games I didn't start. A huge part of it was Todd. He really struggled to get along with other people. I wasn't used to the dynamic of rifts in the team starting with the head coach. Both Jeff Tedford and Belichick had been guys you wanted to work for. Even Bill made up for his idiosyncrasies with a calm demeanor, surrounding himself with the perfect people. Todd just seemed to create chaos.

While I was renting a house in Kansas City, I decided to buy some property in nearby Independence, Missouri. Growing up in Redding, having a place to escape to in the woods was just part of life. When I finally found a piece of land that worked for me, I fell in love. At that time it was like an impenetrable forest. It hadn't been tended to in years, the pond on the property was barely recognizable, and it was going to take a ton of time and effort just to make it buildable.

It was perfect. Just what I needed. The off-season was always a tough time for me, away from the football that had long distracted my mind and kept me busy. For over six months out of the year, the day-to-day structure of football season vanished. Sure, we continued to work out, had some team activities. But my off-seasons in New England were full of sitting around and secret trips to Friendly's. In Kansas City I needed something to do.

The property gave me a place to bury my mind. I wanted to

do as much of the work myself as possible, clearing the land and building a cabin. It would be simultaneously a place to escape and another part of my cover. I'd fill it with beer for drinking, guns for hunting, and invite my teammates and other guys out there to continue to prove just how very straight I was.

By now I was in my midtwenties, not just the starry-eyed rookie new to the league. It was time I got a girlfriend, settled down, got married. With each passing day I was single, I was standing out more and more. While I never got many questions about women, and I had my "girlfriend back home" if I did, the appearance of always being the guy without a woman on his arm weighed on my mind. The cabin, essentially a hunting lodge, would in my fucked-up head give me more cover.

Chapter 9: They Know

Because of the work on the property, I got home to Redding only a couple times that off-season. One night it was just Dad and me headed to dinner in his truck. For me, despite it being a mess for the team on the field, the 2009 NFL season had been the most lucrative of my career. I played in all but two games for the Chiefs that season, and I started all but four. I had just signed a big one-year contract that would land me about two million dollars. Dinner was on me.

My dad had been a bit odd as soon as I got to the house for my visit, just a little more distant than usual. Ever since high school I had been a real source of pride for him. In America, nothing says "real man" like playing football. No matter how many deer a guy shoots, no matter how many chicks he bangs, playing football, and then making it all the way to the hallowed halls of the NFL, tells everyone that you are a strong, powerful, "real" man. For my dad, being able to talk to people about his son in the NFL was almost as good as being in the NFL himself. He took pride in me, and that felt good.

The restaurant he picked that night screamed "real man" too. Market Street Steakhouse is everything you think it would be. Dark wood. Huge selection of beer. And steak. Lots of steak. Walking into the dining room, you could smell the rich flavors of butter and gravy dripping from the walls. I loved that place.

My dad had always been a steak-and-potatoes guy. It was mid-week, and I was happy to see the restaurant wasn't very busy when we walked in. We followed the hostess to a table on the side of the dining room, away from the few people in the place. I almost never talked to my dad solo. If I was on the phone to someone back home, 95 percent of the time it was my mom I was talking to. When I was visiting, I was eating with my mom or both of them. Fifteen years after those family picnics under the redwoods I was still a mama's boy. The distance of big fights with my dad in my teenage years still lingered between us.

Dad had returned to football refereeing, so I knew we had a lot to talk about. Most of the time, football was the last thing I wanted to talk about with anybody. But with my dad, I was relieved to have the topic. He'd really slowed his football officiating years ago to follow me on Saturdays in the fall, but now he was back in it every Friday. By the time I'd gotten to Kansas City, he wasn't coming to any of my games, which was fine by me given the disaster that first season with the Chiefs turned out to be. Hell, it was such a mess I never once invited my parents to a game in Kansas City. Yet all of the football gave us a topic for chatter. After we'd gotten a bunch of the football catching-up out of the way, there was an odd lull in the conversation, Dad staring into his beer.

"Brian came by the house," he told me.

Brian had called me a few weeks earlier just as he pulled out of my parents' driveway, to let me know he'd stopped in for a visit. Brian had known my parents for years, since our high school football days, so normally it wouldn't have been odd. But Brian and I had just had a falling out over a mutual business deal gone bad, so my antennae had gone up when he'd told me over the phone that he had stood around the island in my parents' kitchen chatting with them for a while. Brian could be a bit unpredictable when he got pissed off, and I could only imagine at the time what on earth he had said to my parents. Right after that conversation with Brian I had called my parents and we'd had our very first real "fuck you" conversation. Now that my Dad was bringing it up, I knew there had to be a punch line.

"What was he bothering you about?" I sipped on my way-too-sweet margarita, no big deal.

Now Dad was slathering butter on his roll. A lot of butter and a lot of slathering.

"He told me about you smoking some pot." *Check.* "And he said your moods have been a little . . . erratic lately." *Check.*

If you could picture the most red-blooded of the most blue-collar of the most traditional American guys you know, that's my dad. When he heard "smoking some pot," he probably heard "abusing drugs" and started thinking about Nancy Reagan's "Say No to Drugs" campaign he'd come of age with. Crack dens and drug dealers, like I was on the street corner shooting up with hobos. Like I said before, my dad was proud to say he had never smoked anything in his life. My biggest fear about smoking as a kid had always been what my dad would do if he found out. Even though I was just smoking pot, and taking my team doctor's prescription painkillers when he prescribed them, my dad didn't like it one bit.

"It's nothing to worry about," I said. "Football's a grind, Dad, you know that. Trust me, I'm not the only one smoking to dull the pain."

He nodded.

"Why's he telling you this shit anyway?" I asked.

"Said he was concerned."

Concerned? Fucking asshole.

"Brian's got his own problems he should be dealing with—"

"There's something else," my dad cut in. He lifted his beer and took an extralong swig.

Oh, this should be good.

"Brian said you might be—"

I'll never forget the way he said the next word. There's a famous video of Jim Mora when he was the coach of the Indianapolis Colts answering a question from some reporter about the postseason. "Playoffs?" Mora blurted, simultaneously shocked and offended, contorting his face and his vocal cords into a labyrinth of disgust that lives in infamy. That's how my dad said the next word.

"Brian said you might be—gay??!!?!?!"

Quick, scoff.

I scoffed, let out a chuckle even.

The average closeted guy might cringe at the question. Years earlier I would have. Not *this* seasoned veteran. I hadn't lain in bed for hours, days, weeks, thinking about how to handle just this very situation only to choke now. This was the biggest play of the biggest game of my closeted career. I had spent so much time preparing for this moment, I had virtually seen film of myself sitting in this very seat in this very restaurant with my dad asking this very question over and over and over in my head. As usual, my forehead was already damp with a bit of perspiration, and if my dad had been paying closer attention he might have noticed my nearly audible GULP. He wasn't, and I knew exactly what to do.

Okay, first deny it in a roundabout way.

"That's ridiculous . . ."

Second, put it back on him.

"You know that's crazy . . ."

Third, deny it flat-out and look him straight in the eye.

"I'm not gay. That's disgusting. You think my teammates would tolerate that shit?"

Fourth, discredit the messenger while you take a bite of food and hammer away at him.

"Guess I should have listened to you all those times you told me to stay away from that guy." By now I was calm and collected, deliberately cutting a piece of steak and sticking it my mouth.

My dad half-nodded. "He just said he was concerned about you."

Fifth, go for the kill.

"You said yourself a dozen times, why the fuck would I ever trust someone like him? He's just trying to stir shit up because we had a falling out."

I gave my dad the chance to ask about it more. I was ready and on a roll. But he changed the subject. Years and years of preparation for that question had led me right to this moment, and I earned a fucking MVP award. And the guy I just beat was my dad. He never brought it up again. Talk turned back to football, but by then my half of the conversation was on autopilot. Brian knew. After four years of living together, he was piecing together the puzzle. The trips to Friendly's, the hunting lodge, the guns, the beer, the 330 pounds—Brian had, as I'd feared since our New England days, seen behind the curtain. He knew.

Who else knows? Has he told anyone else? I need to get our fight resolved. He can't tell anyone else.

When I got back to Kansas City, I made two things a priority. First was getting on the same page with Brian again. That old adage—keep your friends close and your enemies closer—suddenly had so much loaded meaning for me. Brian was my friend, even when we got into a fight. But the last thing I could have him doing was sowing the seeds of concern with people about me being gay. As long as were cool, I knew he'd keep his mouth shut about it.

The other thing I needed to do was add some people to our house. It had been just Brian and me living together for far too long. He was chasing women all the time, so I couldn't imagine that anyone would possibly think we were more than friends. But my dad's question set my mind spinning faster than usual.

That off-season I invited a couple of rookies to live with us. Cory Greenwood had been the number three pick in the Canadian Football League draft that year. The Chiefs had picked him up and he needed a place to stay, so I gave him one. Same with Jake O'Connell, a tight end out of Miami, Ohio, whom the Chiefs had picked up in the seventh round of the NFL Draft the year before. They were great additions to the house, good guys who didn't dig into anybody's business. The house was five bedrooms and four stories, so we were pretty spread out and didn't step on each other's toes. They weren't making a bunch of dough so I didn't charge them rent.

The whole situation worked out for everybody. I would help them save money and, in my fucked-up head, they would help save my reputation. We became friendly through that, often taking my boat out on the lake together. They didn't just break up the "two guys living together" appearance, they were also two more pairs of eyes peeking behind the curtain of my life. Even if Brian was going to run around telling people I was gay, I made damn fucking sure those two guys saw me as the straightest dude on the team.

Ding-dong. I was back in Kansas City playing some video games before heading off to the stadium for minicamp when the doorbell rang. The neighbors were often stopping by to take a spin in the go-kart, so I went to the front door ready to let them into the garage. Standing there was a deliveryman holding an envelope.

"Ryan O'Callaghan?"

I confirmed.

"Sign here, please." The envelope was from the NFL. When I got inside and tore it open, life changed on a dime. I had tested positive for weed.

Fuck. Fuck. Fuck!

I had always been incredibly careful with it. Everybody knew they'd get tested for street drugs once a year, either at the start of minicamp or the start of training camp. As long as I stopped smoking the stuff six weeks before minicamp, I'd be home free. As I'd get off the weed I would start to use the team-prescribed painkillers a bit more. As soon as my urine sample got taken, I could start right back up again for ten months. That year I followed the same strategy that had gotten me through my first few years. This time, somehow, the test came back positive.

When I got to the stadium that afternoon, Dave Price, the head trainer, chatted me up about it. Per league rules, from what I was told, there were only two people with the team who were allowed to be informed by the league about a first positive street-drug test: the appointed drug tester with the team, and the trainer. Dave was cool, and I went to the locker room like any other day.

The Chiefs' appointed drug tester tracked me down there. "I need to test you today."

Man, this is no joke.

Once you're in the league's drug program, you no longer get tested once a year, you get tested up to five times a month. And that's not just during the season. In the off-season the drug tester will come to your house, your hotel, anywhere. When you're on the program you have to let the league know when you're traveling and where exactly you'll be staying, so they can send a guy to test you no matter where you are. One time they sent a guy to test me in Las Vegas. A year later, after yet another shoulder surgery, I was staying at one of my buddy's houses east of Berkeley to recover for a few days before heading home. The league sent the Raiders' guy to my buddy's house the day after surgery to test me. *The day after surgery.*

Right after I was put into the program, I had to go to Chicago to be evaluated by a bunch of experts. The league wanted to dig into me mentally and emotionally, understand why I was doing the drugs. Were there personal problems involved? Was I going to be a liability for the Chiefs or the league?

I talked a lot that day to psychologists and psychiatrists about the physical pain of playing in the NFL, something I figured they had heard many times. I stuck to the physical pain and avoided talking about the emotions underlying all of it. I knew they were trained professionals with the ability to dig past the answers I wanted to give. But there was no chance I was going to talk about how the high helped with being a big, fat, closeted gay guy. With their dozens upon dozens of questions, that's the story they were unknowingly trying to get to, but I had long practiced being in a room talking to these very doctors about everything but being gay. It never came up.

Being in the program was a nuisance for sure, but other than forcing me to cut the weed, it didn't have a big impact on my life. Nobody knew I was in the program unless I told them. I had to pee into a cup a bunch. It really wasn't a big deal. But getting caught a second time? That would be catastrophic. Then everybody in America knows about it, suspensions come raining down, and life gets a lot more difficult. Plus, then they start *really* prying into your life. For a guy holding a big secret, there was no fucking way I was getting caught with weed again.

Practically speaking, the potential ramifications of a second positive test did what it was designed to do: it kept me off the weed. Yet an unintended consequence was my sudden need to turn to something else to dull the pain of all the injuries. I had had so many surgeries, so many injuries, and I was still carrying around 330 pounds. I had to find a way to cut the constant pain. Without access to weed, I turned to what the league gave the green light to: prescription drugs. Vicodin. Oxycodone. Dilaudid. In the past, during the six weeks before a drug test, I often ramped up my use of prescription painkillers as I cut out the weed. But that was always temporary before I started smoking again. This was a permanent change. I now had to find ways to get more of these "legal" drugs. I'd find them any way I could.

The positive test couldn't have come at a worse time. I had had a really good off-season with the Chiefs. I won an award from the team for my hard work during those six months of 2010. I even got a primo parking spot for it, right next to the door of the facility. I was going into the 2010 training camp ready to conquer the whole league.

We were doing nine-on-seven drills at a practice in August when a defensive lineman made a move on the right guard and slammed directly into my hip. He sent me into a split, which for a guy my size meant bad news. I knew as soon as I went down that the damage was serious. Tests showed I now had a partially torn groin to go along with all the other injuries.

Suddenly I was dealing with even more severe pain, but the weed was off-limits this time around. The team doc was quick to prescribe me some new painkillers that I happily accepted. I felt like I didn't have a choice. I was a big, tough boy, but the pain of these injuries was just too much to bear without some help. The amount needed by a guy like me to dull the pain was, just starting off with it, double what an average person would take. They also started me on an intensive rehab of blood plate-let injections, or PRP, using a hyperbaric chamber.

About twenty days of rehab after the injury, I hit the prac-tice field again. The season had arrived, and they needed me out there. The first drill of the first practice, the groin tore again. This time it wasn't a partial tear, it was torn right through the muscle. That left me with one of the biggest decisions of my career. I could get surgery to repair it, go on IR, and miss the season; or I could rehab it aggressively and hope to be back on the field by October with a pretty broken but workable groin. I just couldn't go on IR again. If I missed another season with another injury, it could be the end of my career, and the end of my career was the end of my life.

So I opted for the rehab to get me back out onto the field as fast as possible. It showed Scott and Todd that I was dedicated to the team, and that I was willing to work my ass off. It was going to be another month of platelet injections and hyperbaric chambers, all trying to get me back into my starting spot.

I was determined to make a full recovery.

10

Chapter 10: My Coaches and Me

While I was rehabbing my latest injury, the team did well. The other teams we beat weren't exactly the best in the league, but we were still 3–0 and sitting atop the division. Just as I did with the Patriots, I was a religious rehab attendee. Dave Price was as good as anyone they had in New England. Better. I did just what he asked, always a little more if he let me.

Walking the halls one day, riding the wave of the team's success, one of the team's coaches—I'll call him Coach Johnson—was walking with a noticeable limp.

"Hey, Ryan, Dave tells me your rehab is going well," Coach Johnson said.

"He's thinking a couple more weeks before I can get back in, but I'm pretty much ready to go." Then: "How's your leg?"

He reached down and rubbed it for effect. "Hurts like a bitch."

"You have something to hit the pain with?" I asked him. I assumed he would get what he needed from the team doc, but I wanted to help one of the guys making roster decisions if I could.

He told me he had it covered, but thanks.

While I was sitting in the training room later on, Coach Johnson came by again. "Ryan, I could actually use some of that help, if you're able," he said.

"Yeah, no problem. I'll bring it tomorrow."

He patted me on the shoulder and headed off.

The next day, I brought a few Vicodin in a bag and gave them to him in his office. As I put them in the bag I wondered why he hadn't just gone to the team doctor to get some. Doctors in the NFL had handed out prescriptions for painkillers to me like they were working on commission. When I entered his office and handed him the bag, he was in the middle of something and gave me a quick thanks. It wasn't a big deal for me to help him out, and frankly, I was happy to do it.

Despite what I've written, don't let anybody tell you that NFL players don't lose their starting jobs to injuries. While I was in New England I heard this myth over and over again. An "unwritten rule." I foolishly believed it, even on a Patriots team that had switched quarterbacks years earlier because of an injury. When I was told by that very same Patriots coaching staff to go sit back down on the bench because Nick was healthy again, I listened.

When I was ready to come back for the Chiefs in October of the 2010 season, suddenly the rule was erased.

"We've just got a good thing going right now," Todd told me while we were sitting in his office. The team had gotten off to a 3–0 start, then lost the next two. Yet somehow Todd had decided that Barry Richardson brought a good vibe to the lineup, that the gods smiled upon him. It was odd the way Todd talked about the decision, like it was some superstitious voodoo that determined his choice. It was his decision to make, and I accepted it. But just like in my final year with the Patriots, I was determined to win back my starting position.

Opportunity finally knocked the Sunday after Thanksgiving. Our starting left tackle, Branden Albert, got injured and would be out for the game. The team moved Barry to left tackle and put me in at right tackle. I wanted to make the most of it. Even if Todd was going to keep me on the bench, I would make everyone else question that move, maybe even get the attention of another team.

Mission accomplished. We went into Seattle that day and obliterated the Seahawks in one of the toughest stadiums to compete and win in. Matt Cassel threw four touchdowns and wasn't sacked once that game, his best day yet in almost two seasons with the Chiefs. Jamaal Charles ran for like a thousand yards. It was one of the funnest days I ever had in the NFL. Everything clicked.

On the plane ride back to Kansas City that night, I was pumped. I hadn't felt like this since the game against the Giants when it seemed I had gotten the better of Michael Strahan. I had given Todd a lot to think about. If I had lost my starting job to injury, surely he would have to reevaluate his stupid superstition.

We weren't long into the flight when I got a tap on the shoulder. I looked up and there was Coach Johnson, half-smiling. He was often walking up and down the aisle on flights, checking in on guys. I looked down and he had his hand out, like he was trick-or-treating. By then his visits for more Vicodin were not uncommon. I'd stopped asking questions about it—it was what it was. And I didn't feel like I could say no. This was a guy on the coaching staff, and I needed all the support I could get. I reached into my bag, got out a bottle, and gave him a pill. A quick nod and he was on to the next row to talk to more guys.

The whole arrangement was both ballsy and totally stupid on Coach Johnson's part. He even texted me about bringing him some painkillers at one point, being just vague enough so he could have some kind of plausible deniability if I ever brought our little arrangement to someone's attention. I made damn sure to save that text message. He was handing me dirt on himself that was cringe-worthy. Here I was, a player simultaneously trying to crack the starting lineup and keep his spot on the roster, being asked by a coach to give him prescription painkillers.

Also, his getting drugs from me started just as I was accumulating more and more prescriptions. Looking at it from the outside, it could have seemed like my increase in prescriptions correlated with me giving the drugs to a coach, like he'd scripted it himself.

Idiot.

I was thrilled with the relationship, because it gave me leverage over the team. Football wasn't just a job for me. It was keeping me alive, so I was going to fight to stay in the NFL no matter what it took.

Maybe the threat of me going public would buy me a year. But if it came down to saving the team's reputation versus saving my life, I'd blackmail them in a heartbeat.

The next week, Branden was back from his injury and Barry returned to right tackle. I barely played. I felt I still had a lot to contribute to the team, even with my groin injury. I had showed it in Seattle. Unfortunately, the coaches didn't agree. We made it to the playoffs that year, only to get completely destroyed by Baltimore, right there in Arrowhead Stadium.

 **Chapter 11: My Final Off-Season**

You know who didn't lay an egg in the playoffs? Aaron Rodgers. After all he'd had to deal with playing behind Brett Favre and then being the guy who supplanted him, it was great to see my buddy lead the Packers to the Super Bowl. About two weeks after winning the big game, Brian and I went to Vegas to celebrate with him. He was there for a couple of paid appearances and he invited a bunch of his friends to join him. That's when I first met Kevin, Aaron's new personal assistant who I guess was living with him at the time.

At one point we were at the top of the Palms hotel partying like it was 1999. When Aaron was named the Super Bowl MVP, he became certifiable A-list material. Athletic. Smart. Handsome. Smiled a lot. Great personality. Made everyone around him feel good. My high school acquaintance and college buddy was suddenly a superstar. Being around him in Vegas that weekend, it's hard to put into words what that kind of profile might suddenly do to someone.

Yet Aaron was the same Aaron who drank wine coolers on my boat years earlier. We were now just in a VIP booth next to the deejay living the life. The deejay that night was Pauly D from *Jersey Shore*, and Aaron was totally obsessed with the guy's hair. So was America, for that matter. Aaron and Pauly D were like fanboys with one another, both fawning over each other and snapping pics. It was pretty hysterical. At one point Aaron leaned over to the deejay booth and tried to run his hand through Pauly D's hair. He took a couple of the spikes and tried to crunch them down. No dice.

"That shit really doesn't move," Aaron said, laughing.

Aaron wasn't a big party guy, but that night he was enjoying himself. It was awesome for me to see. None of this could have been happening to a better guy.

"You're not in Chico anymore, Bubs!" I yelled into his ear as the music blared. That was a good night.

Months later, Brian and I were in Green Bay visiting Aaron at his home. I was sitting on the couch in the living room flipping through magazines when Brian walked in holding Aaron's replica of the Lombardi Trophy. He was pointing at it, mouth wide open.

"That's not the real one," I said. "It's a replica."

"I'm well aware, but, I mean . . ."

"You get one for winning the Super Bowl, you know."

"Yeah, but do you put it in a box by the trash?" Brian had been in the garage getting a few things organized for Aaron for garbage day. That's when he'd found the trophy Aaron had won just a few months earlier, sitting in a cardboard box next to the trash.

"Oh, *that's* where that went," Aaron said, walking into the room. "Somebody was asking me about it just the other day."

"What is it doing next to the recycling bin?" Brian asked.

Aaron shrugged, plopped down on the couch. "Didn't have anywhere to put it."

He has to be the only NFL MVP in history to have trouble finding a place to put his Super Bowl trophy. But that was Aaron. It was Aaron in high school, it was Aaron at Cal, and it was Aaron in the NFL. The guy hadn't changed at all. And I just loved him for that.

Brian walked over to a shelving unit, shuffled a couple of items, and put the trophy between a bunch of pictures of Aaron and his buddies. "I found a place."

Aaron chuckled. "Thanks."

Before I left we exchanged a couple jerseys. He'd wanted a Randy Moss jersey that I had lying around, and I told him I wanted one of his. I didn't care much about football, the NFL, or the players who played, except for the guys I had friendships with. When he signed his jersey for me, he wrote, *You're a great player and an even better friend. Love, Bubs.* He truly was the same old Aaron. Nothing was ever going to change that.

During that off-season I visited my half sister and her husband, who were living in Lincoln, Nebraska. She had married a Nebraska-born Lutheran whom I had always liked. Hanging around my sister always scared me a little. She asked a lot of questions, all the time. About football, about our parents, about my life. She kept me on my toes, and I always had to have some go-to responses for her that didn't sound canned.

We were all in her kitchen standing around the island when one of their twin boys mentioned that a classmate had come out as gay.

"Well, what do we think of that?" my brother-in-law asked his boys.

They both stared at him and, as if they'd been coached to perform at the drop of the hat, squealed, "Eeeeewwwwwwwwwwww!"

I stood there and watched as their dad smiled and laughed with the kids for parroting homophobia they had obviously learned somewhere. It was like being back at our family picnics, with the men outdoing one another with their gay jokes. I felt bad for those two boys in that moment. I saw myself in them, knowing how it would feel for them if they were gay, being told by society that their very existence is something to be disgusted with. Part of me wanted to take a swing at him for not so subtly approving of the homophobic reaction. Instead, I did what I always did. I smirked like I was entertained by it and kept my mouth shut.

Awful.

The NFL lockout couldn't have happened at a worse time for me. When the NFL and the players' union got into a big fight in 2011 and the players were shut out of the league that March, my lifeline suddenly had a kink in it. Often the first guy in the film room, always studying playbooks, at the facility working out whenever I could—that off-season, the NFL literally told me I couldn't do any of it. Nobody could.

Some of the guys who lived in the area would meet up at a high school and go through workouts together. As the starting quarterback, Cassel would run the show. I had always loved the process of the game—digging into the playbook, the film study, the practices. I could do without the weight training, especially with all of my injuries. But that was part of the drill so I embraced it as much as I had to. It kept my mind busy, and I was also really good at it. Having those few chances that off-season to show up and work out with the guys was helpful to me, even if I doubt it had much effect on our upcoming season.

What I could do was go spend time out at the cabin. Time and money. I decided that off-season that my time with the NFL was nearing an end, so I started spending money like a man on a mission to bankruptcy. When the time came for me to pull the trigger, I wanted to make sure I'd follow through. I figured if I had no money, if I'd spent every penny I had earned, I'd have no choice but to end it all. I wasn't sure if I was going to live for another one, two, three years. What I did know is that I didn't need to save for retirement or anything else. All I needed to live was my NFL paychecks, because I wouldn't be around for long after my last NFL game. So I poured my money and my mind into making that property amazing. I spared no expense, putting about seventy thousand dollars into building that little cabin. Hell, I installed marble countertops. Not many cabins have marble.

I bought my own tractor so I could do a lot of the work myself and with friends, clearing land, building roads, and yeah, planting trees with Brian and Dustin. I didn't hire a general contractor, I would read on Google how to do stuff, and my neighbors and friends would come out to make sure I wasn't totally screwing up.

I wasn't an idiot, though, and I hired a few professionals to build some really nice cabinets and do the finish molding. I knew my limits. But almost everything else, from building a makeshift storage area for the tractor and ATVs to pouring the footing for the cabin to putting on the roof, I did it all with the massive help of some wonderful friends who would always come through. I would spend hours and hours on my tractor clearing the property, the dogs chasing me around. It was a good project to distract me a little since football wasn't available. The solitude kept me addicted to that place.

 **Chapter 12: Completely Addicted**

That's how I ended up in my cabin that night, Brian and Dustin headed to the fish store, me inhaling narcotics and polishing my guns alone but for the dogs, the melancholic tunes of Jason Aldean filling the air. And yeah, getting high on OxyContin.

When the cabin was finished, it was beautiful. I actually took a lot of pride in that place, and it showed. I would spend literally hours mowing the property every couple of weeks. I'd get on top of the mower, grab a six-pack, take a hit of the Vicodin, and mindlessly move my way back and forth across the property, losing myself in the whirring of the motor. The trees we planted that day were the final touch. My crypt was ready.

I never really came close to actually killing myself that off-season. The thought of playing another year with the Chiefs, and earning back my starting spot, kept me going. I still had a competitive nature. I still wanted to beat the other guy to the top. I felt I'd deserved more from the Patriots and the Chiefs during my time with each of them.

As the lockout neared its end and football was again on the horizon, I was trying to convince myself daily of just one thing: *I still have more to live for.*

One day a few weeks after planting the trees with Dustin and

Brian in 2011, I wake up with more anxiety than usual, and that's already a lot. All of the fears that have been churning in the back of my brain have come to the fore. The drugs I'd gotten introduced to at Cal, and then reintroduced to with the Patriots, have all sunk their claws into my soul. Each morning I never do anything before my trip to the bathroom for my "fix." Today, though, I go right to the front door to find . . . nothing.

Fuck!

I rush to the bathroom, take an eighty-milligram oxycodone out of the medicine cabinet, and stick the pill in my mouth. It has a hard, sweet coating that I have to suck off the pill first; the coating is tough to crush and no fun to put up your nose. When the coating is gone, I put the pill on a plate and crush it into dust with a quarter.

Ahhhhh.

Snorting the powder calms me down before the rush. Mental peace. I've long since stopped taking the shit just for pain—this is about getting fucked up. Every morning. Every day, all day. I snort the oxycodone every three to four hours. If I have a team meeting at Arrowhead Stadium I take a little less; if I am home all day I take a little more. I pop a handful of Vicodin when the high isn't enough, and then a Dilaudid when I need more on top of that. I have access to enough drugs on a monthly basis to kill several men.

I stare into the mirror, my eyes heavy but happy. The two voices on my shoulder chime in.

What the fuck are you doing with your life?

Fuck it, they did this to you.

"They did this to me. Fuck it."

I pick up the phone and dial. No answer.

A few months earlier I had been talking with a buddy in California and I mentioned not being able to get all the painkillers I needed. Figuring he was just helping an NFL buddy deal with the pain of playing football, he told me about a connection he has. When I want more, I can give him a call and send him a thousand bucks. A few days later UPS delivers a small box to my doorstep, and inside will be a bottle with a hundred Vicodin pills. On top of all the other prescriptions I am filling, this rounds everything out nicely and gets me what I need.

I cannot fucking believe they won't just let me smoke some pot.

I know my guy is still asleep on the West Coast, but I need a tracking number. Delivery time. Something. I need to know that the package is coming. I only have enough stuff for a few more days.

Rodger and Taylor are pacing in the living room. We'd gotten Rodger after Brian and I moved to Kansas City. Taylor needed a buddy around the house when I was at the stadium and Brian was gone. She had terrible separation anxiety. When we left her alone in the house, even for an hour as we headed to the grocery store, she'd tear shit up. She loved to devour sunglasses. I lost at least two wallets to her choppers.

It wasn't any big inconvenience getting a second dog. Once you have one dog, a second is no more work. And my bed can fit all three of us. They always want to sleep with me. We had driven all the way to Detroit Lakes, Minnesota, to get him after I found him with a breeder. He is gorgeous and a total sweetheart. I named Rodger after Aaron, just because I thought it was hysterical to name a dog after him. And I didn't want to name a boy dog "Bubbles."

Their pee time has to wait for my dose, but I can never make them wait too long. Those dogs keep me alive. "Come on, guys."

They barrel out the front door and race onto the lawn. They

have their pre-pee routine, checking the yard for squirrels, cats, anything they can chase. The adrenaline is their morning drug of choice.

"Hi, Ryan!"

The voice from across the street answers my prayer. My neighbor Karen, just getting out of her SUV, is waving at me as her husband Rick moves toward their front door on his crutches. He had surgery on his knee a few days ago.

I wave back, thinking about my next move as I walk across the street. I am, frankly, a celebrity in the neighborhood. And I am a great neighbor, if I do say so myself. I've always felt I should give back to the people around me. Since I'm spending money like I'm going to die, I've bought some crazy shit. I picked up a go-kart the whole neighborhood can use to spin around the local streets. I have two boats that I use to entertain the neighbors on the local lakes. I even bought this wacky mobile barstool the guys get a total kick out of.

Plus, every Fourth of July I spend thousands on fireworks and set them off in front of my house. Everything is legal in Missouri. These aren't little sparklers or firecrackers. I'm talking about box after box of four-inch mortars. They shake all the windows in the area, but nobody cares because they are all in the street with us drinking beer and watching the display. When I go to places like Vegas with Aaron, or anywhere in New England with a guy like Matt Light, I see what "star treatment" is really like. In those cases I always blend into the background while my bigger-name friends get all the attention. But here, in this Kansas City suburb where I am starting to slowly kill myself, I am the star who is always giving back to the community. I figure I'd rather they talk about that nice, generous guy they all love hanging around with than wonder why I don't have a wife.

Still, I can't just walk up to Karen and pop the question.

Looks odd. Feels odd. But I know Rick has some good painkill-ers in the house from his surgery. I have to get some.

Play it cool.

"Karen, how's Rick?" I ask as we walk toward each other, never any traffic to worry about.

"Doctor says he's healing nicely. The pain's going away a bit, so that's good."

Bingo.

She opens her arms to me as I get to their curb. Hugging isn't really my thing, because it always means I'm bending down to get to someone else's height. But I would do a cartwheel and a split if I had to.

"Yeah, I've been dealing with this shoulder thing forever."

"The stuff you men go through for your sports."

Damn, now what?

Then: "You know, the doctor gave him a bunch of painkill-ers, but I don't want him taking them anymore since he's feeling better."

"I did run out, and my shoulder has been killing me this morning, but . . ."

"Wait right here."

Standing there on the curb of my neighbor's house as she hunts for drugs for me, I am both excited and disgusted. I'll have another day's worth of the drugs, just in case the shipment doesn't show up.

But it's not enough. As the lockout continues, I'm finding it's never enough. I am sinking more and more money into pre-scription narcotics. I have nine monthly refills from the team doctor for painkillers in one month. Nine! Think about that. Every injury, every surgery, they just keep writing another pre-scription for another painkiller. Some of them are opioids. You know what else is an opioid? Heroin. The NFL is cool with me taking some cousin of heroin, but I can't smoke pot. I don't know if that's racist or classist or just plain stupid, but it's something.

I have different-strength Norco prescriptions from the team. I have Dilaudid from my last surgery. The most fucked up part? With the way the prescriptions are written, I can get vast quantities more than any regular human should ever get. I have my guy sending me stuff on a regular basis. Yet even all of that's not enough.

Where else can I go?

One afternoon I stop into an urgent care facility right off I-70 looking to sit down with one of their doctors. I tell her who I am, and that I play for the Chiefs. I tell her the pain is just unbearable after all of my surgeries, and that the team simply isn't giving me what I need.

"Doc, I can't be honest with them about how much pain I'm in," I tell her, "or they'll know I'm in worse shape than they realize." I also flat-out lie to her about the amount of painkillers the team is giving me.

That does the trick. She prescribes me thirty-milligram oxycodone and sends me on my way.

This is too fucking easy.

Chapter 13: Dear Mom.
Dear Dad.

By the time the lockout finally ends and training camp opens, I am getting high on painkillers every day, all day. I've seen it before. When I got cut by the Patriots, Nick Kaczur had gotten caught with a fuckload of oxycodone. The feds reportedly got him to help nab his dealer. No fucking way I'll ever do that to an old friend in California helping me out. I'll just shoot myself before I squeal on him. I'll end my life before I end his. Besides, it's their own fucking fault that any of us want to use the shit anyway. Nick has already flamed out with the Patriots, his career over. I feel like they cut the wrong guy, but I guess everybody does.

Now here I am doing the same exact thing Nick did that ultimately led to his career being cut short. This is the power of these drugs that the NFL encourages its players to use. They are so addictive and so good at masking pain that you'll forget every lesson you've ever learned about not using them. All the conversations I heard at the NFL Rookie Symposium are completely erased, and all I can think about is where I'll get my next hit.

Even before training camp I know I have lost some mobility with the groin injury. My quick feet have always been one of my assets, and suddenly they just aren't as quick as they were. I have also lost some of the power in my legs. The way to compensate is to use my back and shoulders, but my shoulders have been through multiple surgeries already.

Halfway through camp that season I am in a one-one-one drill when the guy opposite me pushes my arm over my head, just like Ty Warren had done a few years ago. I know as soon as I hit the ground that my season is over before it even starts.

Not again. Please, not again.

The team training staff gets me into the training room and does some quick tests. It isn't good. It's the same pain I'd felt during my final injury with the Patriots. Again the shoulder has dislocated out the back.

I lie down on a training table, my shoulder wrapped in ice, trying to control the swelling. Practice is just letting out, and guys are streaming into the training room. Scott Pioli is among them, and he walks straight for me.

"Hey, Ryan, how's it feeling?" My eyes say what my mouth can't, my mind stopping the words before they can form. I fear that those snaps at practice today are the last ones I'll ever take in the NFL. I have had so many shoulder surgeries. Hand surgery. Injuries to my knee, my neck, my groin. I've had concussions, even blacked out. At twenty-eight years old my body is completely falling apart.

I try again to respond. While the words won't come out, this time the tears do. Scott puts his hand on my shoulder to comfort me.

"It's okay," he says. "We'll get you back out there." Scott knows that's a lie. He came by because he knows. In that moment, though, his little offering of hope makes me feel a little better, even if I don't really believe it. He's one of the good guys in the business who truly cares about people other than himself, and it always feels good to have him around.

A few days later, the Chiefs put me on injured reserve. For the second time in four years my season is over in training camp. Scott calls me into his office to talk about it. This time, he's more realistic. "This might be it for you," he says. He knows what the deal is. My legs had saved me as my shoulders deteriorated, but now with the groin injury a season ago, my legs are failing me too. They can't cut me during the season, since my injury is football-related. Scott tells me it's going to be tough to keep me on after the season. He can't be my friend with roster decisions, he has to be the Chiefs' general manager. And as the GM, he knows I'll likely end up right back on IR the following season too.

Frankly, I don't want to cost the team a bunch of wasted money anyway. I'm not that guy. I already signed a "split contract," which means that if I'm injured I will get only part of my salary. Every other contract I'd had with the Patriots and Chiefs came with a full salary for an injury. But we all knew I was a potential liability for the team, and getting half a salary this season is the absolute least of my worries.

The ride home after that meeting with Scott is a tough two miles. I have built my life around football in a way few other men do. It isn't my passion, it isn't a stepping stone to stardom; I'm a big fat offensive lineman. Instead, football is my lifeline. Football is my hiding place, it is my beard.

When I finally get home that night, a bottle of Maker's Mark in hand, I hole myself up in my room. I picked up my prescription for more painkillers before I left Arrowhead Stadium, so on top of everything else I have, I'm good to go for the night. I know I'm not supposed to mix alcohol with Vicodin, and certainly not hard alcohol like whiskey, but I just don't give a shit. If I pass out from all the downers in my system tonight and slip away into a forever sleep, it will end up saving everybody a lot of headache.

Halfway through the bottle and a few pills in, my phone rings. It's Mom. I stare at the phone buzzing on the bed next to me. Mama's boy always picks up her call, every time. No matter how I'm feeling, her voice puts me in a better mood. Now, I feel the need to protect my mom from myself. Whether I die tonight from drugs or in a few weeks from a bullet to my head, I know I have to start pushing my parents away. Losing me is going to hurt enough as it is. So much of my plan to kill myself has been in motion for a couple years—the cabin, the guns, spending money like it's growing on trees. Putting this next part of my plan into motion is going to hurt the most. I figure if I can create some distance between my parents and me, it will soften the blow to them, particularly my mom, when they get the phone call that I'm dead. I have been used to talking to my mom at least weekly. Sometimes we've gone weeks chatting almost every day. Now, for her sake, I have to cut that all off.

It starts now.

The phone finally stops ringing. I wait a minute, staring at the phone, wondering if she'll call again, hoping she will and hoping she won't, all at the same time. The phone sits silently. No follow-up call. I tear up again. Crying like a fag.

This is actually the end.

I scratch Rodger's head—he and Taylor have followed me into my bedroom like they do every night—grab the bottle, and sit at my desk. I take another swig and dig into the nightstand for a pad of paper and a pen. I've thought about this moment for years. I stare at the lined paper, pen in hand. How do you start a suicide note?

Dear Mom, I write. Then I pause, considering the next words. I know what they're supposed to be, but it feels awkward just thinking about writing them. But I can't not write them. *And Dad.* At that desk that night I scribble a bunch of stuff—*I'm sorry, please don't be sad*—that I truly want them to think. I don't want them to blame themselves, even though I know they may not be able to help it. It isn't their fault. Did I grow up in a home that didn't make it very easy to be gay? Sure. Would they reject me if I told them who I really was? Of course. But this is on me.

Over the next few weeks I take out that pad of paper, scratch out some things, write some more. It's usually at night, when I've sunk myself into the beer or the whiskey, and some of those precious pills too. I don't write a single word of that suicide note sober, but I know exactly what I'm writing. Through all the erasing and rewriting of that letter, I never tell them the real reason I need to kill myself. I will never come out to them, or anyone else, in a note or in person. I don't want anyone to know that all along I've just been a faggot in a football uniform. Even in death, I have to be the straight guy.

After this latest shoulder injury, I spiral down fast. I'm taking an absurd amount of painkillers, up to thirty pills of various strengths on an average Tuesday. Now I'm hell-bent on draining my bank account. There are days I spend four hundred dollars on the prescription narcotics the NFL has deemed okay. For real.

I never dip into recreational drugs, though. In my fucked-up head I have to keep abiding by the NFL's rules. I am still getting tested regularly for street drugs. The craziest part of all? I'm still holding onto the glimmer of a hope that I can return for the 2012 season and keep myself alive. At the same time, I am completely sabotaging any chance that could possibly happen.

By day I keep going to rehab at Arrowhead. I am still always one of the first people into the training room. But I'm often not much more than a walking zombie. The drugs completely fuck up my sleep schedule. Eight hours of sleep don't exist anymore. The drugs, and my racing mind, wake me up early and often throughout the night. I won't go to bed until two? Three? Then wake up after sunrise, get my early-morning hit, and I'm up, up, up!

Despite living with Brian, Corey, and Jake, and going to Arrowhead nearly every day, nobody says a word. Corey and Jake have their own shit they have to take care of just to stay on the team, and Brian is always off being Brian. Besides, I have been training myself to put on an act my whole life. Now, controlling myself when I'm around other people, while still floating somewhere around Jupiter, is easy. Or so I think. The truth is, I'm getting careless. I'm doing so many drugs so often that I start to forget about hiding it. I'm high all the time on opioids, and even I can't hide my head spinning with the planets.

Half the team must know I'm a drug addict.

By night I am constantly thinking about when to finally pull the trigger. I know how I'm going to die, and I know *where* I'm going to die. *When?* is the only question. I get very close a couple nights to just saying fuck it and doing it. When I get in that headspace I call someone I know. The only one who picks up every time is my friend Ted. He's married, has a stressful venture-capital job, but he always picks up the phone when I need him most. Toward the end, I get really honest with him about my plans to kill myself. I confide in him that I want to die. When he asks why, I tell him I can't say. He respects that and listens and tries to console me. I tell him I hate my life but I don't have the courage to just end it.

Getting my suicide note right is important to me. The last people I want to hurt are the people I love the most. A few weeks into the season, sitting on my couch, I have begun to create vivid fantasies of killing myself. This is no longer some far-off concept that I'm doing some long-term planning for. The thoughts in my head are forming into present, concrete ideas about exactly how that day will go, how I'll get to the cabin, what I will do when I get there.

I visualize it during the day . . .

I wake up in the early afternoon. The night before was a long one. I had always planned on throwing a big party my last night on earth, a last hurrah. I love throwing parties for people, but this was the biggest one I've ever hosted. About a hundred people showed up—friends, some teammates. Nobody asked what the occasion was, and even if they did I'd already planned to tell them it was just a celebration of life. I spared no expense, with a really good local barbecue joint catering. I even hired a couple bartenders, got a band, and lit off some of my signature fireworks. The neighbors didn't mind. Hell, they were all there.

Just like every other day, my first move is to the bathroom for my hit. Today I'll make sure I'm as high as possible. I spend most of the day with the dogs. Of all the beings I'm leaving behind, they're the ones I feel the most sad about. Caring for those dogs gave me a reason to live some days when it felt like I had none. We play extra long outside in the yard, tossing the ball around and playing some tug-of-war. Boxers, even gentle ones like Taylor and Rodger, love tug-of-war. I give them extra food for lunch. I know they'll be in good hands with Brian. I totally trust him to take good care of them. They already spend half of their time with him and sleep with him some nights. Knowing they'll be with someone who knows and loves them gives me some solace for leaving them behind. A few hours later I give them both big tear-filled hugs and kisses on their heads. I'm going to miss them, even after I'm dead. They are right now the best things about my life.

I get into my pickup truck and head out to the cabin one last time. Late afternoon is the best time to do this. It's when I'm always the most high and the most depressed, every day. I'm really high now. I have always checked my intake before getting behind the wheel. I don't mind if I kill myself at this point, but I sure in hell don't want to take anyone else with me. I drive extra slowly, even under the speed limit most of the time. I could just pull over any time and take care of business. I always have a loaded and concealed handgun in the truck. Missouri lets you do it, so I figured arming myself was a good idea. You never know where you could find trouble. Yet the cabin was going to be my crypt from the first day I found the property.

I pull into the property and remember how special it's been to spend a couple years out here. So many great memories polishing that diamond in the rough. The lake is so pretty now, cleared of trees on one side and the koi taking care of the algae. There's a gentle breeze blowing through the willows. By now the sun is setting—it's late autumn and the days are getting shorter and shorter. Watching those long, beautiful limbs swaying gently in the wind as the last rays of warm sun dance through them calms me a bit.

As I step into the cabin my eyes wander, inspecting this place I built for the last time. It's so incredibly peaceful. No dogs barking, no traffic. Just the solitude I had sought so many times before. I flip on a light and toss my keys on the counter. I don't want to lose my nerve or lose my high, so I crush a pill on the marble counter like I've done so many times before. One last hit to get me through it. Ahhhhh. Peace. I don't want to spend a lot of time in the cabin thinking because I don't want to question anything I'm about to do. The more time I think, the more likely I am to see the next sunrise.

I go to the gun cabinet and know exactly what to select. The first gun I ever owned was a Heckler & Koch forty-caliber pistol. I bought it right when I was of legal age to own a gun. Even if I didn't love hunting, I've always been really comfortable around guns. Today there will be no accident. I want to have in my hand the gun I am most comfortable holding. Everything this day is about comfort and peace.

The last thing I want to do is screw up killing myself. If I jump from a bridge or a skyscraper there is the possibility I could survive and be paralyzed the rest of my life. I have taken enough drugs to kill myself so many times, so I know that won't work. I have a ridiculously high tolerance to them, and every time I do too much, even for my own body, I throw it all up. Drugs are out. Hanging myself? I'll break the rope. Nope, using a gun seems like the safest and smartest way to do this. I can't fail at suicide. All of the attention and all of the questions afterward would be horrible.

I take the HK out of the cabinet and make sure the magazine is fully loaded. I'll just keep pressing the trigger until I can't anymore. I don't expect to need a second shot, but I want to be prepared. I take the note to my parents out of my pocket and set it on the little coffee table in front of the couch. I've spent countless hours working on that letter. In about two days they'll hopefully forgive me for being distant the last couple of months.

The couch is a big part of the plan. I'm at peace with my decision to do this, and I want to make sure I'm completely comfortable for it. I know there will be moments of hesitation before I pull the trigger. I figure if I'm lying down on a comfortable leather couch, I'll be more likely to go through with it than if I'm standing up in the middle of the kitchen. I want to go through with it. I need to go through with it.

I lie down, swing my right leg onto the couch, and use my hand to pull the left one up, another reminder of my broken-down body. I make sure to lie down so I can face out the front door. Another part of the master plan is to be able to look out those gorgeous glass French doors at the willows and the lake. The sun is now giving the property its last kiss of the day—it's perfect.

My heart is pounding a bit. Even if my mind is ready to die, my body isn't. It knows what's coming, and it's revolting.

I can feel my heart beating in my chest. If I weren't high on the drugs, with my mind at peace, my body just might win the day. But nothing's going to stop me from going through with this.

My mind loses its way, starting to spin with a little doubt:

Do you really want to do this to Rodger and Taylor?

Is this the right way?

What will my parents say?

What kind of chicken am I?

I stare out the French doors and lose myself in the trees.

The slowly undulating branches are hypnotic in their movement.

A few clouds in the sky rest behind them peacefully.

I raise the pistol to the side of my head, pressing it against my temple.

The wind. I can see the wind in the trees.

The sunlight is gone. Just the darkness now coming over the lake.

Greens turn to brown turn to black.

And those trees.

They'll stand there forever.

Watching over the place.

Watching the dogs race around the lake.

BANG.

14

Chapter 14: Someone Has Been Watching

I pull into the parking lot at Arrowhead like I have every morning of rehab. There are only a few cars there ahead of me, mostly coaches and some staff. Even with rehab, I want to be the first one in the building. For the Chiefs to have any thought of keeping me around another season, I have to give them a lot to consider. And if I go before anybody else is there, I'll get everything done faster and can then go home to get higher.

When I walk into the training room it is empty as usual. Empty, that is, except for Dave Price. I don't think I've ever been at the facility when he wasn't there. He is another one who cares not just about doing a kick-ass job, but about the guys he works with. He would try anything to get you better, even some wacky voodoo shit. Best trainer I ever saw. And a great guy. Given all of my injuries since arriving in Kansas City, I've spent more time in Dave's room than most. He's been here with the Chiefs for a bunch of years, so he's spent lots of time with plenty of players. Despite all those names and numbers sitting on his training table, he still has a way of making me feel like I matter most when he's working with me.

The way Dave's office is set up, he can look out at the whole training room, clear across to the doors. He wants to know who is coming and going out of his room, what's wrong with them, and how they're going to fix it. He sees me come in that morning and waves me over.

Dave's office is great. So many little knickknacks, little shark figurines, funky posters on the wall. Dave is half football trainer, half hippie, stuck somewhere between the summer of '69 and the Reagan era. He always has good music going, stuff from the eighties, on a giant stereo that's older than me. It's early morning, so Sade is keeping the mood relaxed.

"Shoulder improving?" he asks.

"Arm's still attached, so it's a good morning." I sit on a chair opposite him.

"What are you taking for it these days?"

I give him insight into a tiny sliver of just a couple of the painkillers I'm using. I figure he doesn't need to know about the rest. Funny thing is, he already knows.

"Ryan, I can tell you have something going on." Dave is direct. Always direct. Identify problem, communicate solutions. That's his job.

I so don't want to talk about this.

"I'm working on it. You know I'm in here every—"

"I've been in this league for thirty years," Dave cuts in. "I've seen injuries, divorce, gambling." He looks me in the eye. "Drugs."

I stare at him, my jaw cocked to the side.

"You know I'm not talking about your shoulder," he says.

Of course I know. All my life I've cut off communication before it can get deep—keep it surface level or move on. In all his years working in the NFL, he's seen plenty of big fat guys injured and downing as many pills as they can get their hands on. But I can't let him in. I always have to fake it.

"The shoulder hurts like hell, Dave."

He sits back in his chair, nodding. He knows I've had nine

prescription refills for painkillers. And he's seen me acting like a fucktard the last couple months.

"There's somebody I think you should sit down with, Ryan."

"I don't need to talk to anybody." I'm getting pissed now. *This isn't my fucking fault.*

"I just need to get my damn shoulder fixed."

Dave sits in his chair watching me. The drugs are really taking over now. He's gotten under my skin by calmly giving me advice and looking out for my best interests. What a jerk, right?

"Her name is Susan Wilson," he says. "You won't be the first or last guy I've sent her way. Talk to her. She's helped a lot of guys who find themselves caught up in stuff they never intended."

I tell Dave I don't want to go see any stupid shrink, and he assures me she is on the up-and-up.

For ten years I've been plotting how to kill myself when football is over. The note is ready now, I just have to drive to the cabin, leave it on the coffee table, and that will be that.

That morning with Dave, I sit there looking off into space and nodding. I have always been the big, strong giant who can put away brewskies and crush things in his bare hands. Dave sees through all of that right into the psyche of a human being in pain, who's completely lost all control. He has tossed me a lifeline. Not a contract, not an offer to play football, not a way to hide—a real lifeline.

"What's her name again?"

I hate Susan Wilson within minutes of meeting her. She is my complete opposite: a well-put-together tiny little black woman from the South whose main purpose is to get inside my head, figure out what the hell is making me turn to drugs, and expose my every secret to the Chiefs. I look at her just like

I've looked at every defensive end I've ever gone up against.

She is the enemy.

What's worse, she has this demeanor about her, this way of using silence that I've never experienced before. I'm not good with silence, and she figures that out right away. She just keeps being quiet, waiting for me to spill my guts.

We are like oil and vinegar. And I am definitely the vinegar. It's not so difficult to understand how a six-foot-six, 330-pound closeted redneck might not take kindly to her. Except the crazy thing is, by my second visit I start to trust her. That silence she uses, her way of listening, quickly overpowers me. Everywhere I've been my whole life has been designed to make me hate myself. Family picnics. Family fights. The high school locker room. Our house in college. The NFL. The cabin. All I have ever felt from every place I have ever been is that I am wrong for being me, I am bad, and I need to die.

Dr. Wilson is different from everybody I have ever met, in so many ways. She isn't just a clinical psychologist to me. I am still getting high every few hours of every day. I am still going to rehab, trudging through the halls, trying to avoid Dave Price so he doesn't ask any questions. Nothing has changed in my life, except I see in her the possibility of maybe, eventually, if everything works out perfectly and we have a cone of silence, telling her my secret of secrets.

As I continue to visit with her a couple times a week, I find myself letting my guard down little by little. She is Brian Urlacher, Ty Warren, and Michael Strahan all rolled into one. She knows exactly how to get past my best blocks, convince me to step aside, and say, "By all means, go sack my quarterback."

About a month in, it gets to be too much. She gets too far inside and I don't like it one bit. Leaving one particular session, I know that the next time I sit down with this woman, I will let her all the way in. And I can't have that. So for about a month I cancel a string of appointments with her and ramp up my drug intake even more. I'm not ready to do what I know I have to do. This is one of the most conflicted periods of my life. I have believed since I was a kid that I can never tell anyone my dark secret. Now this stranger has me rethinking that, swinging between inspired moments of possibility . . . and dark nights of drunken self-hatred.

This lasts until one morning when I wake up sweating more than usual. I have a meeting with Dr. Wilson scheduled for that afternoon. Like I have all month, I pick up the phone to cancel. The dogs are lying on the bed, and Rodger slides over and licks my face. The dogs. Whether I am fucked up on drugs, have a bad game, or just want to be alone, Rodger and Taylor are always so happy to see me. Other than the drugs, they have become the only constant in my life, the one thing I can count on to make me feel good.

Lying there in bed that morning, Rodger licking my face and snorting all over the bed, their love hits me. All of my great plans about ending my life after football have never properly taken them into account beyond the notion of Brian looking after them. These two dogs who have come to mean so much to me. Do I want to live? Yeah. I just haven't figured out why. Staring at the dogs that morning, I realize I want to live for them. I stare at the phone in my hand, and I put it back down. I rub Rodger's face. This crazy dog. I lie there for a while, my painkillers calling for me. I get to them eventually, and yeah, I increase the dose that morning. All morning. All afternoon.

Just stay high.
Don't worry about it.
Stay high and talk to her.
Or just fucking pull the trigger.

E-fucking-nough already!

All day I keep as busy as possible. Go to Arrowhead, have a rehab session to end all rehab sessions. Get my car washed. Stop at the grocery store. Go to the cabin. Putz around there. By late afternoon, it's time to head to my appointment—or not. I had grabbed the note when I left the house. The light is hitting the tops of the trees, kissing the day goodbye. I sit on the sofa with the note in my hand. I go to the counter and crush a pill, inhale it. It never takes long to hit.

Today's the fucking day.

Do I stay? Or do I go?

I meet Dr. Wilson in the early evening as we always do, after her official office hours. It's the middle of fall so the sun has already set. She knows the NFL guys need discretion, so we don't meet at her office, but at some school for kids with disabilities, a quiet spot where she has access to some space. When I pull up in my truck, she is there in her car, waiting for me.

Damn.

I haven't snorted a thing in almost an hour.

I gotta down this Vicodin.

"I started to wonder if I'd missed another cancellation," she says.

I kind of enjoy the little bit of snark out of her. She's earned it.

We go inside and I walk straight for the bathroom where I can snort the stuff.

I can't lose the high right now.

When I finally walk into our meeting room, she is sitting there thumbing through some notes. I figure she's annoyed with me after all the cancellations, now making her wait for me once again. She couldn't be more professional.

"How have you been since we last talked?" she asks.

I sit down across the long boardroom table from her.

"You know, same."

She pauses, looking at me, studying me. I am spacing the fuck out, can't stay focused on her. My eyes are everywhere.

Fuck, did I overdo the pills? She knows. She has to know.

"Tell me about your day . . ."

Fuck this.

"Okay, I need to tell you something," I say.

She sits back, her eyes laser-focused on mine, like she is some Jedi working one of her mind tricks.

I stir in my seat. I can barely sit up straight; the drugs are shooting through my veins, electro-charging my whole body.

Stop fucking dragging this out.

"I gotta tell you something I've never told anyone," I say. "And you can't tell anybody, right?" That is my biggest paranoia, that she will tell someone at the Chiefs and all hell will break loose.

"As I've said, I cannot legally discuss anything we talk about," she responds.

"Not even the team?"

"Not even the team," she assures me. Then leaning in, gravely: "But if I believe your life is in imminent danger, I am obligated to intercede." She knows my life is on the line. She knows.

I have cried by myself so many times, so many nights. All of it is bubbling to the surface now. Even with the drugs pulsing through me, I can't suppress it. Tears spill down my face. This big behemoth of a man crying in front of this woman. I feel embarrassed, but I can't stop it. Every time I open my mouth, I am consumed with thoughts about all I have been through. The drugs. The guns. Pretending to date women. Lying. Practicing lying. It's probably a good thing I'm high, because there's no chance I would say anything more if I were sober.

"Dr. Wilson . . ." I focus really hard, staring at the table. The blank table. No distractions.

Say what you gotta say.

". . . I . . ."

She sits there patiently, not saying a word, that fucking silent game again, waiting and waiting like she has so many times before. Silence but for the buzzing of the fluorescent lights and my quivering body.

Just fucking say it.

"I'm . . ."

Say it, you faggot!

Deep breath.

"I'm gay."

I feel like I'm hyperventilating, struggling to breathe. I've never said those words aloud to anyone. Not even myself. I cover my face with my hands, hoping to crawl into a hole and die. Tears are streaming out of my eyes now. I am at the same time relieved to finally share my truth, and ashamed of the words even as I say them.

What the hell did you just do, you fucking idiot?

Dr. Wilson doesn't say a thing at first. She just sits there, watching me blubber like a fucking faggot. Then: "That took a lot of courage, Ryan."

I look up at her, this sheepish expression on her face. She gets out of her seat, walks around the table, and wraps her arms around me. All my life I have told myself that people will hate me if they know the real Ryan O'Callaghan. I'd have to kill myself if they knew. This woman, a stranger just a couple of months prior, hugs me. She's supposed to hate me, but she hugs me. It takes a lot more strength to be honest with myself, about myself, than it does to lie. It took awhile to build up that strength to tell Dr. Wilson. In that little classroom that evening, she meets that strength with strength.

"I want you to know," she says as she walks back to her seat, "that you're not the first NFL player to sit in that chair and tell me that very thing."

The tears are slowing now. I pull my hands away and look up at her.

"You're not alone," she says.

To know I'm not the only one isn't a shock. I had already heard Esera Tuaolo talk to us at our Rookie Symposium years earlier. Still, hearing that she has counseled another gay player, maybe not so long before I sat in that chair, gives me a glimmer of hope, like this particular woman has been sent to me by some greater power. And I don't even believe in that hocus-pocus shit.

After that the floodgates open. I tell her about the cabin and all the guns. I tell her about the drugs. She already knows about some of the painkillers, but this time I tell her everything. And I tell her about the suicide note, just waiting for the wrong moment.

But telling some stranger I'm gay doesn't suddenly change the outlook I have embraced since I was a kid. The life of a gay man is still not worth living, the people closest to me will still hate me for it, and I am still going to have to end it all.

"Why?" she asks. "Why do you assume you have to kill yourself?"

I start telling her about being a kid in Redding. The isolation of those family picnics. The constant jokes I heard from the men in my family about being gay. The shit guys said in the Enterprise High School locker room all day, every day. Forget about the messages in the media or the lack of role models. The people closest to me told me constantly, from my first memories, that I was straight and gay people were bad. I share with Dr. Wilson that all of this has translated in my head into *gay people deserve to die*. Whether or not that's what they said, that's certainly what I heard.

"That was a long time ago," Dr. Wilson says. "How do you know your parents will reject you, their son, today?"

In so many ways, adults and their parents fail to know each other, clinging to a past that they all left long ago, but that they assume the others still live in. When I go home to visit, my mom makes me meals I loved as a kid. Yet my tastes have changed. I love her for making my "favorites," yet she doesn't really know what my favorites are anymore. But my mind isn't ready to believe they have changed their thoughts about gay people, even if twenty years have passed.

"I just know," I reply.

"So you're just going to end it all without ever testing your game plan?"

She's good. If you make it all the way to the NFL, you know a thing or two about developing game plans, the importance of running them by people and testing them at practice. She knows that one way to get through to a guy like me is to appeal to the sense of reason instilled in me from a decade of organized football at the highest levels. She convinces me that adjusting my game plan makes a lot more sense. Why not go home, tell my terrible secret to my parents, and then if they have the reaction I expect from them, at least I will know before I put a bullet through the barrel of one of those guns.

When I get back into my truck that night, the tears become a river right there in the parking lot. Telling Dr. Wilson my secret fills me with just about every emotion I have ever felt before or since. Anger. Worry. Fear. Hope. All my life I have been living with my own personal thoughts about being gay. Just telling her feels like a million pounds off my shoulders. This is the very first time I have ever been totally honest with someone about myself. And it has only taken twenty-eight years.

Twenty-eight fucking years.

More than just being two ears to hear me, Dr. Wilson is helping me see that maybe, just maybe, all of that stuff my dad and my uncles and so many people around me have said about gay people might not be how they actually feel. She helps me see that if I am suddenly the gay person they are talking about, they might change their tune. For the first time in my life, it seems possible that all those jokes in the park as a kid weren't actually about me at all.

If I am going to go all-in and come out to my parents, I feel like I need a test run. I want to come out to someone who's been in my life, who knows me from back in the day, who's known the asshole Ryan who stampeded through the halls of Enterprise High. Brian is the perfect choice.

Except, there is now so much baggage with Brian that it could fill a garage. First, let me be super clear: Brian is just about the least gay person I have ever met. His is the proverbial picture in the dictionary next to the word *straight*. I have always worried about how he might react if he knew because we have been attached at the hip since college. We are "Ryan and Brian." We live together. We travel together. We have tried to start a business together. We are best buds. And I am so afraid that he will freak out at me being gay because people might wonder if he is too, like maybe we are more than just friends.

Plus, there were those incidents with him: asking me on the Jersey Shore if I was gay and then telling my parents that he thought I was. But then again, he only told my parents when he was looking for a weapon to use against me after we had a big fight. Still, if this is a weapon in his eyes, things won't go well when I tell him.

Our relationship has also been fracturing for some time. We are, even before he knows the real me, drifting apart. Getting into arguments, even weeks-long fights. He'll have every reason to kick our friendship to the curb if he has an issue with me being gay. Telling him will be a big test.

A few days after my cryfest with Dr. Wilson, I walk down the stairs to find Brian in his room on the lower level of the house. We shoot the shit for a minute like we always do and then I cut to the chase.

"There's something I gotta tell you. And there isn't an easy way to say it, so I'm just gonna say it."

Brian's expression is priceless. Eyes wide, mouth cocked to one side. If I weren't so nervous, I would probably laugh.

"I'm gay."

As odd as his expression was before I said it, his reaction now is that much more reassuring. He is like a soldier ready for a fight, suddenly realizing the person coming around the corner isn't the enemy.

"I'm sorry I didn't tell you before, but I just didn't know how," I say.

"It's okay," he replies. "I kinda knew anyway. Not in a bad way. I just knew." He then steps over to me and gives me a hug. "Love ya, bro," he says, just like he always has.

What the hell was I so afraid of?

Living so closely with him for so many years has given him plenty of glimpses behind the curtain. Living with Brian has always seemed like the perfect cover, me with this very, very straight guy. Yet at the same time I knew deep down that I wasn't doing enough to keep him guessing. No matter how many times I had quietly disappeared to Friendly's for a couple hours, Brian already knew.

His reaction sitting in the basement quiets the questions I had leaving Dr. Wilson's office. Good or bad, I am now determined to come out to my parents.

15

Chapter 15: Getting Caught

It's a few days later and I have packed some stuff into my Dodge Ram Laramie ready to hit the road for California. I am now a man on a mission. Nothing else in the world matters other than sitting down with my parents and finally having "the talk." Nothing, that is, but the drugs. Addiction doesn't just disappear after a few sessions with a psychologist. I am still getting up in the morning, taking my hit, and hitting the day. I am never going to be able to quit abusing these pills as long as I am still in the closet. As far as I am concerned, I am still very much in the closet with a future completely in doubt.

I have a whole bag of drugs with me when I get in the truck. The Vicodin and the OxyContin, of course. The Oxy is my drug of choice when I can get my hands on it. I want to keep a gentle high all the way to Redding so I don't lose my nerve. I'm taking along some Adderall too, just to keep me awake for the drive. When I get behind the wheel, I have a weak buzz. I know enough not to get flat-out high if I'm going to drive 1,800 miles straight through.

I'm cruising down the road listening to Jason Aldean when my phone rings.

"Ryan, it's Dirk. Where are you?" Dirk Taitt is the head of security with the Chiefs. Cool guy. Really professional and always good to me.

"Just got to Nebraska," I tell him. "Driving home to California to see my parents." He doesn't need to know why.

"You gotta turn around, Ryan."

Fuck! Dr. Wilson told somebody! She fucking told me she wouldn't. Fuck!

"Why, what's up?" I play it cool.

"I just got a call from the Independence Police Department in Missouri," Dirk says. "They have a package in their possession they need to speak to you about."

Fuuuuuuuuck.

I know exactly what he's talking about.

"Just go to the police and answer every question they have," Dirk says.

I am already looking for the next exit. "Dirk, what should I tell them?"

"The truth," he says. "Just tell them the whole truth."

As I drive back south on I-29, I imagine what I'm headed for. Handcuffs. Jail time. Court hearings. Only a few days earlier I had suddenly found the will to live, and now it is all going to come crashing down on me. I wonder if they have been to the cabin. Have they found all of the guns? Did they find my goodbye note? They have obviously identified who I am if they reached out to Dirk. Now I could be walking into a trap.

By the time I get to the station Dirk has called the detective, who is waiting for me on the front steps. I get out of the truck, walk to the detective, and shake his hand. I thank him for meeting with me. I don't know what else to say. They caught me. They have the goods. Now it's up to them what they do with it all. He escorts me through the station with just about every eye on me. *There goes the six-foot-six NFL player about to get thrown in prison.*

When the detective opens the door to a small interrogation

room, there's the box sitting on a small table with not a lot else in the room and some pretty bright lights. It's just like you'd see in the movies.

"Have a seat."

I walk around to the other side of the table and sit in the chair. I'm sweating now pretty good. I'd grabbed a few napkins from the truck to dab my face. I knew I'd need them.

"Does this box look familiar?" the detective asks.

"I can certainly guess what's in it," I say.

He reaches into the box and takes out a big pharmacy bottle. There's no hiding its contents: the bottle has the word *Hydrocodone* printed right on it. He unscrews the cap and dumps the hundred pills onto the table. I get the little yellow pills. They're the best ones.

I nod. My latest shipment of Vicodin was supposed to arrive at the house the day before, but it never showed up. I had called my buddy that morning and he told me he'd shipped it a few days earlier. I was so anxious to get on the road that I didn't think much of waiting around for it. When the detective asks me where I got it, I tell him almost everything. What I don't tell him is that I have dozens and dozens more pills in the truck sitting right there in their parking lot. And not just Vicodin. I have it all.

"How much did you pay for these?" he asks.

"A thousand."

"So your buddy's making a profit."

"No, no, that's what he gets 'em for."

His tone turns. "Why are you lying for this guy? These pills cost three dollars apiece here in Kansas City."

Now the drugs are talking—I have a nice buzz going—and I suddenly decide to get lighthearted. "Three bucks apiece? Tell me where and I'm there."

Unbeknownst to me, the police in California are knocking at the door of my buddy's house at the same time these guys are grilling me. Dirk had told me to not contact my buddy, and now I know why. The police in California seeing a phone call come into my buddy from my phone as I'm driving to the police could cause a whole heap of other problems.

I had told my buddy to send the pills through UPS. I didn't want to use the post office, because in my head that would be using a federal agency to transport the drugs, and I figured that would be a lot worse. So every few weeks he went to a local UPS center and shipped my package to a UPS location in Independence. Along the way, somebody got suspicious of this guy sending this same-shaped box to me on a regular basis. When they opened the box, the label on the bottle said it all.

As we are spilling our guts, the two police departments are apparently communicating with one another. Thankfully, my buddy tells the complete truth too, and our stories match up perfectly because of it. Lying about almost everything in my personal life has become second nature to me, but on that day telling nearly the whole truth gets me through.

After a couple hours of grilling me, they let me go. Don't ask to search my truck, don't ask to search me. Instead they just . . . let me walk right out the front door. It's a good thing, because I know I'll need a nice buzz to get me to California after all that. If they had searched my truck, I probably wouldn't be walking to it.

I come to find out they had a search warrant all drawn up to go into my cabin and house and turn them upside down. Before they went out to my property, though, they figured out I played for the Chiefs and gave Dirk a heads-up. Dirk had vouched for me, told them I'm a guy worth saving. There is a ton of weed at the house, some of which I've shared with teammates. It's always delivered to a neighbor down the street so Jake and Cory would never get caught up in it if someone got suspicious. If the police had gone to the house that day they had me down to the station, they may have ended up uncovering more about the Chiefs roster than they wanted to deal with. But I talked a lot with them that day about my plans to head home to California and get clean; I said that I had turned a corner and just wanted to be off the stuff. They respected that, and they respected Dirk.

Thank god.

I will never hear about that bottle of pills on the interrogation table ever again.

16

Chapter 16: On My Deathbed

I waste no time getting back on the road. The whole ordeal with the cops has set me back a few hours, and darkness is on the horizon. As soon as I get back in the truck, I throw down a couple painkillers and an Adderall to bolster my nerve and keep me awake. I plop a thirty-two-ounce container of Diet Pepsi in the cup holder, grab a big bag of Sour Patch Kids from the gas station, and I'm on my way. Country-music stations across Nebraska and Wyoming keep me company as I drive through the night along I-80.

Driving in the dark, alone in the truck, my mind does cartwheels about my family. I go back into my childhood memories, trying to find moments—reasons for hope—that maybe I'd assumed wrong all along and my parents will welcome their gay son with open arms. It is hard to find that hope. Yet Dr. Wilson's words keep spinning in my head: *Why don't you find out if you really have to kill yourself?*

Every few hours I pop another Adderall, along with my usual unhealthy dose of Vicodin. I can't let the drugs wear off. In a fucked-up way, if it hadn't been for a solid high the day I met with Dr. Wilson, I'm not sure I ever would have come out to her. It was only in an altered state of mind that I had the nerve to say those words, "I'm gay." Sitting down in my parents' living room and telling them I'm gay is going to be the hardest thing I've ever done in my life. I can't do any of it sober.

By the time I get to Nevada, there's a problem. I have been driving for eighteen hours straight, right through the night, and my heart is speeding up pretty good. At first I'm just feeling a bit off, like all the drugs had just taken a left turn. It makes sense. I've been washing down the Sour Patch Kids with nothing but caffeine and drugs. My parents' house is another eight hours away, but like two-a-days on a hot Berkeley afternoon, I know I can push through it. But before I can get much farther, I feel downright sick. Suddenly nauseous, having trouble focusing on the road. And my heart is pounding out of my chest a million miles an hour. I don't have to touch my chest, I can feel it booming inside me.

I Google the nearest hospital on my phone and speed my way to Battle Mountain General Hospital in the heart of the Nevada desert. When I pull up into the parking lot, the hospital is about the size of a gas station, perfect for a town of three thousand people, but I can barely fit inside myself. I walk in the door and spill my guts about the drug use to the first person who will listen. The doctor seems unfazed. He tells me that because I am essentially a newbie to Adderall and have taken it only a couple times before, I'm not used to the effects and I'll be just fine. I am encouraged by what he has to say. He's right, I've never popped three or four Adderall in twelve hours, on top of all the caffeine, sugar, and the other drugs. It's a lot, even for me. So I sign a couple papers and they send me back to the road.

My intention is to go to my parents' house in Redding first, but by the time I get to California a few hours after the hospital visit, my heart is totally out of control. I'm sweating even more than normal and I feel like shit. My uncle John lives in a little town called Graegle, in the middle of a beautiful national forest northwest of Lake Tahoe. When I was a kid, one of Uncle John's favorite pastimes was cracking jokes about gays. I'd never let on to him that it bothered me, and I'm not going to be blabbing about it now. But I realize I need a place to lie down and rest. Driving, at this point, is a terrible idea.

When I walk into his house I look like a swamp monster. I'm covered in sweat, I haven't slept, and I'm simultaneously high as a kite and ready to crash. My half sister is visiting them, and I don't mince words. I feel like shit, like my heart is going to explode. When a 330-pounder says his heart's going to explode, everybody gets concerned, even when it's a twenty-eight-year-old professional athlete.

Uncle John is a former firefighter, so he gives me a once-over. Before he can get through half of it, I tell him I need medical help. My sister hurries me to her car sitting in the driveway and takes me to what is more like a couple of trailers with some medical equipment than a hospital.

Fucking idiot, should have stopped in Reno.

When I walk through the door, a very nice nurse calmly asks me to sit on a chair as she takes some of my vitals. She asks what's going on, and I tell her about the combination of drugs and driving through the night. She wraps a blood-pressure sleeve around my arm, pumps it up so it squeezes around my bicep, then slowly releases the air. She looks down at the gauge and the calm expression on her face quickly transforms. She stares at me, fear in her wide eyes, her mouth agape. She yells out for help.

Oh shit.

All hell breaks loose. A handful of people rush into the room and help me onto a gurney. They are all talking really fast in hospital-speak to each other, hooking me up to seemingly every machine in the place. They don't wheel me into another room, they are bringing the machines to me, like they can't lose a second of time. Seemingly everyone in the place is hooking me up to something, asking me questions, taking more tests. It's a frantic scene. One of the doctors tells me they need to get my blood pressure and heart rate down right away. "Just do everything you can to relax," she says, "and focus on your breathing."

They make me down some nitroglycerin. They hook me up to IVs and monitors beeping and blurping as fast as my heart rate.

I panic. All of my adult life I have been very ready to die. If death had come my way, I would have accepted it as the inevitable end of a life that was never meant to be lived. Yet over the last few days I have suddenly wanted to live. Dr. Wilson has instilled in me a curiosity about all of my assumptions over my entire life. For truly the first time, I have some semblance of hope that all these years of planning my death weren't necessary, and that I can continue to live after football drifts into my past.

There I am, ready to spill my guts to my family after living with a secret identity all these years, plotting to kill myself rather than tell them, and I am going to die of a drug overdose hours before I get to tell anyone. I'm going to die with my secret, as I'd planned all along.

Fuck, I don't want to die.

Those first couple hours in the hospital are the longest of my life. Truly. My aunt and uncle have come to the clinic to be with me. I'm not sure what to do with my secret. I am at the point now where I want to tell them, but how the hell do you share something like that while you're on your deathbed? After holding in my secret for so long, I have to say something. Right there, hopped up on a bunch of drugs, my heart racing like a jaguar, hooked up to a bunch of machines in the middle of the national forest, I tell them I'm gay.

They're quiet, staring at me. They didn't see that one coming.

"Oh Ryan," my aunt says, getting emotional, "we don't care about that."

Lying there under the bright hospital lights I brace for the worst from my uncle. This is the moment of truth.

"Just tell me you still like country music," he says. The same guy cracking gay jokes and accidentally making me feel like shit as a kid is now the guy using jokes to make me feel better about myself.

They keep me in the hospital for two nights. My heart rate and blood pressure do eventually come down. The worst of the drugs wear off, and they release me from the clinic the next night. I go back to my uncle and aunt's house and we have a long talk. My aunt doesn't care about me being gay at all. It really seems like a nonissue for her. My uncle has a lot of questions, but he keeps it light with his humor. This time none of his jokes are mean. They don't make fun of gay people. They're kind and fun. It's Uncle John's way of telling me nothing is going to change between us.

Shit. Maybe Dr. Wilson was right after all.

While me being gay is a piece of cake for them, what they are deeply concerned about is the drug use. The doses I am taking on a daily basis would literally kill most people. I don't hold anything back at this point, and I describe to them a lifestyle that you only read about in the obituaries. Uncle John has always been very antidrug. Even when he has surgery he avoids prescription painkillers because he knows how they fuck with your mind and can lead exactly where they have led me. But he knows I can't just stop them cold turkey, and that it's going to be a long, arduous process to get off of them. He makes me promise I'll stay there with them for a few days while I start on that process.

A few hours after finding out I'm gay, here's my uncle mapping out a plan to save my life.

I don't have much choice but to go along with it. For days after being released from the hospital I have chest pains. But this isn't your average dull pressure. Every time I breathe I can feel it, like my lungs are filling with tiny shards of glass. The people in the clinic hadn't overreacted when they flipped out at my blood pressure. I was damn near dead when I walked through their doors. They eventually told me I had kind of a cramp in my heart from overexertion on that drive due to all of the drugs and not sleeping. If I leave my aunt and uncle's place, I'll be seriously risking my life. For the time being, after their reaction, I don't want to do that.

The only request I make of my aunt and uncle is that they don't say anything to my parents while I am staying with them. I don't want my parents to know I was in the hospital, or that I'm in California. I have pushed my parents pretty far away. If I am with my aunt and uncle for a few days, even a week, and my parents don't hear from me, they won't think anything of it. My uncle agrees, but he tells me he doesn't want to have to lie to my dad. The two of them talk on a regular basis, so I have to agree to going right home and tell my parents everything as soon as I'm well enough to get behind the wheel again.

Deal.

A couple days later my uncle and I go back to the hospital for a checkup. The fire alarms around my health have finally quieted. My uncle makes sure we talk with the doctor at length about a specific plan to wean me off the drugs. The doctor gives me a prescription for regular-dose oxycodone, which to me is like baby aspirin. I haven't been dealing with the fives and tens most people take, I'm downing the thirties and eighties. I literally won't even *feel* a five-milligram dose of the stuff at this point.

But this is what I have to do—slowly take less and less until I can get through a day without taking any at all.

As my unbearable chest pains subside in the coming days, my ability to fall asleep does too. Each day is less opioids and less sleep. Despite having masked the pain for a while, I still have my physical injuries. The Chiefs still have me on injured reserve after a half-dozen shoulder surgeries and a torn groin, among so many other problems. The pain wakes me up at two a.m., then three a.m., then four thirty . . .

Plus, I now have more thoughts and questions racing through my head than ever before. The last few weeks have gone so quickly, and they have turned my life upside down. Other than helping around the house, I don't have a hell of a lot to do while I'm there. My mind is in overdrive.

I also feel horribly sick. Stepping down with the drugs hurts. Taking less and less each day doesn't eliminate the withdrawal symptoms, it just limits them. While my body is getting past the drugs, my mind still wants them. Badly. Thankfully, the doctor has given me some medicine to deal with the withdrawal too, but I still feel it.

On top of the heart issues, tests come back showing that my liver is in serious trouble. Even with all of the drinking I had done in high school, college, and the NFL, there had never been any sign that my liver was ailing. Now it is. The doctor says it isn't beyond repair, but it's getting there.

These fucking drugs.

But the NFL says pot's the big problem.

I never once cheat on the plan the doctor presents to get me off the pills. Not once. My aunt and uncle lay down the law with me, and I follow it. I can't thank them enough. I know not everyone has family like that. After almost two weeks my doses are virtually zero. Though the withdrawal symptoms linger and I still want the Vicodin, I am ready for the next big step.

I call my parents' house and tell my mom that I will be coming by for a visit the next day, and that I have something I need to talk with them about. It's an awkward conversation on the phone—it's probably the second time we've talked in as many months. But when I hang up the phone, there is no turning back. I am about to put Dr. Wilson's big game plan to its biggest test.

Chapter 17: The Longest Drive

The drive from Graeagle is about three hours. It winds through some of the most beautiful mountainous woodlands in America, dumping out into a golden valley where Redding awaits. I can't get through it fast enough. I don't even listen to music on the drive. It's the first time I've been sober in over a year and my stomach is turning inside out. I just want to get to my parents' house, spill my guts, and figure out if my living in fear has been for naught.

When I walk into the house, it's like a funeral. By then I look like a normal human being, but my phone call the day before has set off alarms. There are quick hugs all around and then we head to the living room. They sit on the couch together, and I'm on the chair. Nobody wants to wait any longer for the news.

Today I haven't taken a single pill. It's the most dreaded moment of my life, and I am going to do it sober.

Here goes.

"I'm sorry I haven't been in touch much," I start, "but honestly, I've been getting ready to die."

Tears roll down my mom's cheek.

"But it's something that's been inside of me all my life. Something I've been so scared to talk to you about."

My mom is typical Mom: "Ryan, you can tell us anything." She's told me that a million times since I was a kid. Maybe every mom does. But there are things you just don't talk to Mom and Dad about. This is mine. I've spent nearly two decades plotting to avoid this very moment, sitting across from my parents on our living room couches, telling them a secret they don't want to hear. But now it's something they *need* to hear. They need to know. And I need to tell them.

"I'm gay."

Three . . . two . . . one . . .

I look up and my mom is now full-blown crying. My dad just has this blank stare on his face. There is always this moment when someone shares a secret with someone else, like a change of direction. You can't just drive a car forward and then throw it in reverse. You have to stop first. This moment, the three of us sitting there staring at one another, is that brief stop. Then the direction changes.

My mom gets up from the couch and wraps her arms around me. She's given me a lot of hugs over the years. This one is the tightest, like she's hanging on for dear life. "That doesn't matter to me, Ryan," she says through the tears. Turns out she's assumed I was coming to tell them that I have a terminal disease and am going to die. After that twenty-four-hour emotional roller coaster, her son being gay is the least of her worries.

After a few seconds my dad gets up and hugs me too.

"I love you, son."

That's about all my dad says over the next few hours. Heck, he doesn't say much more my entire stay there, which lasts just a couple days. I don't blame him for being quiet with me. His NFL-playing son, the man's man who is carrying on an O'Callaghan tradition of masculinity, just told him he's gay. That he doesn't curse at me and throw me out of the house is, in my mind, a small miracle.

* * *

That night I unload on them about the drugs, my close encounter with an overdose, the hospital, and my two-week stay with aunt and uncle. I also tell them about my plans to kill myself, how I have spent myself damn near into bankruptcy so that backing out of doing so would be that much less desirable. Whatever issue they might have with me being gay is gone with the realization that I have been planning to end my life over it all.

Most of the conversation has nothing to do with me being gay and everything to do with keeping me alive. I feel like I can tell them anything right now. I may be in trouble, but I'm alive. Tonight that is all they care about.

All my life I'd assumed they'd rather have a dead straight son than a gay son full of life.

How did I get this so wrong?

I keep asking myself that question my entire stay with them. It haunts me. Coming out to my parents is all so much less eventful than I had built up in my mind. Is it perfect? Hell no. They aren't perfectly comfortable with it either, especially my dad. But they both know what my alternative is. No, Dad isn't jumping up and down in celebration, calling his friends and relatives with the good news. But I had imagined it being so very much worse than it is.

All those years hearing my dad and his buddies say cruel things about gay people suddenly take a turn. My mom's stories about the doctor doing drugs and dying of AIDS don't change her love for her gay son. Along the way I had missed something. When my parents told me as a kid that I could tell them anything, they had actually meant it all along. When they told me they loved me no matter what, they meant that too. In my closet filled with fear I had failed to hear what my parents were really telling me all those years, my mind getting turned around by some stupid jokes and bad stories. It had never occurred to them that they were telling their son they wouldn't accept him if he was gay, but that's what I was hearing.

Parents have to say the words to make their kids believe it—"If you're gay, I will still love you just as much." And they have to say it over and over. Growing up, our whole world tells us to be straight. Short of my parents specifically telling me it was okay if I was something other than straight, I'm not sure their messages of love and understanding would have ever gotten through. If a parent doesn't actually say the words "It's okay to be gay," their kids will never hear it.

It finally gets through to me that night. When we sit down and they have the chance to express their love for their gay son, they do just that. Suddenly, for the first time in my life, I don't have to kill myself.

Now what the fuck am I going to do?

18

Chapter 18: The Rainbow Tour

In my six-year NFL career I have made about four million dollars. Now, at the end of the 2011 season, I've spent damn near every last penny. I have gone through about fifteen cars. I bought a fishing boat on top of a wakeboard boat. And then there's the massive gun collection. All of it is totally unnecessary.

My financial planner could never make heads or tails of it. He would regularly call to talk about slowing down my spending, putting more into investments and savings. But I always thought I could never get to the day where I would outlive my NFL career. I didn't want to. So I had long ago stopped answering his calls. I wasn't going to tell him what was up, and nothing he could have done would have prevented me from pursuing this path of self-destruction. He has power of attorney, so he could have actually stopped me. He has never invoked that privilege, but I imagine he's thought about it. None of it is remotely his fault or anything he has done wrong. If he had gone that route, I would have found another way. I was hell-bent on spending myself into a forced death.

Yet here I am, at the end of my NFL career, and I suddenly want back in on life.

Thankfully I have assets. As soon as I get back to Kansas City from Redding, I put the cabin on the market. There is no greater symbol of my downward spiral than that cabin. I love it out there, but I simply don't need it in my life anymore. It's worth more liquid than standing. That will put some much-needed cash in my bank account.

I also have a couple vehicles, a couple boats, and some other possessions I sell to bring in money. The new plan is to get rid of almost everything I have in Kansas City and move back to Redding to live with my parents for a while. That will save me a bunch of dough and give me a spot away from any big cities to build a foundation for my new life.

Plus, as it turns out, my financial planner has been somewhat secretly sticking a few of my bucks under the proverbial mattress when he could. I am grateful to have a little bit of savings when it is all said and done.

Driving back to Kansas City from Redding, I have a lot of time to think, and for the first time in a couple years I am thinking like a sober person. One of the things that comes into focus is this sudden need to explain to people that the Ryan O'Callaghan they've known for so many years isn't quite the real Ryan O'Callaghan.

Almost every gay person goes through this. I think it's one of the things that makes coming out so difficult. Even if the lie is warranted and you have good reasons for telling it all your life, you still have to let people know that you've been deceiving them. It doesn't feel good saying it, no matter who you are. That conversation—the process of sitting down and telling people one by one—is simultaneously liberating and painful.

I realize that there is one way to get around all of this: I can talk *publicly* about being gay and *wham*! Everyone will know. But I'm also very aware that there is no chance I am remotely ready for any of that, or for the attention that would come my way. If I am ever going to do anything like that, it will have to wait.

Still, I do know there are a lot of people in my life who need to know. If I am going to start living the life of a gay guy, it is going to come up. I need to have the sit-down conversation with some people, and a lot of them are in football. Given the reaction of my parents, my uncle, and my buddy Brian, if a former teammate or a coach turns his back on me because I'm gay, I can live with that.

One of the people I have to tell in person is Scott Pioli. He and I have more than just a business relationship, we've become friends. We have two big things in common that we've discovered in Kansas City. For one, we both have our issues with Todd Haley. The rift between the two of them isn't a secret. What I know is that Scott is incredibly kind to me, and I never once felt like I was being "spied on." Haley, on the other hand, has acted like a paranoid nut from the day I met him and is the worst head coach I ever played for. So yeah, Scott and I have bonded a bit over some issues with that guy.

He and I had also dealt with the heavy drinking of family members. The topic had come up one day when I told Scott that I was struggling a bit with alcohol, and he didn't hold back. He shared his family's troubles with the same issue, and he opened his door to me any time I needed help. For whatever reason, he had trusted me with his deepest secrets, even as I was lying to his face. He also knew that I'd been seeing Dr. Wilson and that probably meant I either had major psychological problems or there were drugs involved. Now, with that all behind me, he has to finally know the truth.

Soon after I get back to Kansas City, I call Scott and ask him if I can come in to talk to him about something. When I walk into his Arrowhead office later that day, my head is down. I'm moving slowly, both terrified of his reaction and still dealing with withdrawal from the drugs. He comes around his desk and

190 ⊖ My Life on the Line

gives me a hug, like he so often has. Scott's a hugger. We get into some small talk, like one often does before dropping the hammer. But I know why I am there, and I cut to the chase kind of quickly. I tell him that I'd gone home to California for a few weeks, and that I'm now sober. He looks physically relieved by the news. Like I said, he's dealt with alcoholism in his family, and he knows where that can all lead.

"I've got something else I need to tell you," I say, fighting back tears. This is the next big test in my coming-out tour. His reaction will either slow it down or speed it up.

"I'm gay," I say, now with tears rolling down my face.

Scott looks at me like he's at a crosswalk waiting for a green light. Then: "So what's the problem you wanted to talk to me about?"

I've just said the two words I have dreaded most all my life, and his reaction is . . . nothing.

"Scott," I say, "I'm . . . gay."

"I heard you the first time, Ryan. So what's the problem?"

I honestly don't know what to make of it. Is he mocking me? Trying to ignore what I'm telling him, like it never happened? I share more about my life, how this has always been my biggest fear. I tell him about my suicide plans, how I have used football to hide my truth. He sits there, listens to all of it, and tells me over and over that he totally accepts it, he totally accepts me, he loves me, he supports me, and that if there is anything he can do for me, all I have to do is ask.

"You're also not the first NFL player to tell me this," Scott says.

I'm actually more shocked by his support than I was by my parents' reaction. Scott Pioli is one of the most powerful men in the most macho sport in America. He represents the epitome of what it is to be a "man." And here he is, expressing not just tolerance of me, but outright undying love and support. He is also the second person in a month to tell me that I'm not the first gay NFL player to come out to them. I start wondering if I am the only person in the league who doesn't have a network of gay players at their fingertips. I ask Scott if he'd known all along that I was gay.

"Ryan, how would I have known?"

"Do you really think I like coffee that much?" I say. Another blank stare. I explain to him that ever since getting to New England, I always headed right to the training room after every practice. And if I didn't need a trainer that day, I would sit there and drink cup after cup of coffee, simply to buy time while the other guys got in and out of the showers because, in some fucked-up corner of my mind, I had convinced myself that I didn't belong in the locker room when my teammates were getting naked.

Now it's Scott who's tearing up. "I had no idea," he says. "I'm so sorry you felt you had to go through all of that. I had no idea."

We talk for another half hour or so, mostly about football and my future in it. Rather, lack of future. Scott makes it clear that he can't sign me with all of the injuries, despite how much he would like to. It's not a surprise, and I can't blame him. My body is officially cooked. As we get up to say goodbye, the hugger comes around from behind his desk and opens his arms to me. I stick out my hand. Scott recoils.

"What's with the handshake, dude?" he asks.

"I just told you I'm gay," I mutter under my breath.

He's having none of it. He grabs my hand and pulls me in for a hug. It actually, truly, really doesn't matter one bit to him that I'm gay. Not one bit.

"Dude, it's okay," he says. Then, in his signature sense of humor, "Just don't grab my butt."

I laugh. Just like with my uncle, Scott's humor seals the deal. We are going to get along just like we always have.

"Don't worry," I say, "you're too short and bald for me. You're not my type."

Shortly after I leave his office, I call my agent. He doesn't need to bother looking for a spot for me. My time in the NFL is over.

After Scott's reaction, starting the conversations gets a lot easier for me. I tell Dustin Colquitt over the phone, and he is nice as could be about it. Dustin has always been a great guy and a good friend, but he is also a devout Bible-thumping Christian. So I had been nervous going into the conversation. He makes it super clear that me being gay won't not affect our friendship in any way. Months later, when the Chiefs are playing the Oakland Raiders, Dustin takes me to dinner with Ryan Succop, the Chiefs' kicker, and the long snapper, Thomas Gafford. It is three of the most religious guys on the team . . . and the gay dude. And it doesn't matter to them one bit.

The last person I feel I have to have a one-on-one conversation with is Aaron Rodgers. I have told my whole family and all of my close friends, except for Aaron. Every single one of them has responded with incredible support. After telling my parents, and seeing their reaction, I wonder what the hell I have been so afraid of all those years. That sentiment builds more and more every time I tell someone else my secret, so by the time I try to tell Aaron, I have come to assume he'll be equally supportive.

I've been having trouble getting ahold of Aaron via phone for a while. It isn't anything unusual. When you're a Super Bowl MVP and the quarterback of one of the league's most storied franchises, there are a lot of people trying to get your ear. It's the summer before the 2013 season, and Aaron and the Packers are again at the top of everyone's list of expected Super Bowl contenders.

When I finally do get to talk with him, I don't really want to come out to him over the phone. Of everyone in the NFL, I've known Aaron the longest and I've known him better than I've known anybody else. I want to tell him face-to-face. But I also don't want to have to wait weeks or months until I have the chance to see him again. So I do tell him right there on the phone.

"I still love you, Tool," he says. Same old lovable Aaron. He tells me that he wants to see me, and that he'll fly me over to a Packers game that season to hang out. We settle on their November home game against the Bears.

Yet again, someone I once thought would end our friendship if he found out I was gay could not be more perfectly nonchalant about the whole thing. And this isn't some random player, this is one of the faces of the NFL telling me he couldn't give a rat's ass. When we hang up I'm left shaking my head once again.

What the hell was I thinking all those years?

It turns out the Bears and I make a bad combination. On the very first drive of the game, Aaron rolls out to his right and is taken to the ground by the Bears' Shea McClellin. When Aaron gets off the ground he's wincing pretty bad. An X-ray in the stadium explains why: he broke his collarbone on the play. That's the last action he'll see for over a month. Nothing but bad luck.

For the rest of my visit with Aaron, it's just him and me staying at the house. He's single, and he has recently severed ties with his friend and personal assistant Kevin. The end of their friendship seems abrupt. They were as close as I've ever seen a client and assistant get. Hell, one year they had a joint Christmas card with a jokey letter included that made it seem like they were a happy married couple. But I never really felt much of a connection with Kevin, and frankly, I was just glad to spend some solo time with Bubs.

As it happens, I've severed all my ties with Brian too. During a recent houseboat trip on Shasta Lake near Redding with a bunch of friends, Brian got into a big argument with one of our high school buddies. The friend, who had completely accepted me since coming out, called Brian a "faggot." It was eye-opening for me, seeing that word coming from a straight guy who had been incredibly supportive of his gay friend. I also saw how that word could be like a match to a bomb. Brian exploded at our friend, swinging at him with all his force. When I grabbed Brian and restrained him, he turned around and took a swing at me. Our friendship ended that very night.

For both Aaron and me, our best buds and housemates are now both gone, and for the first time in a long while, we get to hang out, just the two of us.

After the game Aaron needed some groceries so we stopped at the local Piggly Wiggly. No matter where we are or what has happened, Aaron is always the same Aaron. Down to earth, making jokes, interested in the people around him, shopping for chicken breast and potatoes. I asked him if he wanted me to get the groceries for him so he didn't have to deal with fans pestering him.

"I got this, just watch me work," he said with a smile and a wink. Sure enough, he walked in, greeted the cashier, and worked the crowd. With Aaron it isn't an act. It's real. With him it's always real. The people in Suamico, where he lived at the time, about fifteen minutes from Lambeau, had also gotten used to seeing him around town. Walking through the grocery store, seemingly everyone wanted to wave hi, but they also pretty much left him alone. He was like one of the townies.

I make chicken piccata and mashed potatoes for us. After dinner we sit in Aaron's living room and talk about life, two college buddies catching up. We don't talk much about me being gay, but that isn't because Aaron doesn't want to. It just seems like a complete nonissue for him, much like it has with Scott. We talk about my next move in life and the financial trouble I've put myself in, a guy who's made millions now living in his high school bedroom with his parents, getting his life together and fighting the NFL to take care of his injuries. Nobody's fault but my own—I just wish I had thought through what I was doing a little better. Aaron is awesome as always, listening intently, processing what I say, never judging and always looking to help.

"You know, there might be an opportunity for us here," he says.

My ears perk up. Aaron tells me that he is looking for small businesses to invest in, to diversify his portfolio and bring in some additional income. He says that if I can present him with an investment plan for a business, and if it checks out, he'll go in with me. He tells me he has gone in on certain businesses as a silent partner with other friends, and he would do the same with me. He puts up the money, I put in the time and commitment.

I've been living in Redding for over a year, with no income. It's one thing for him to tell me that nothing will change because I'm gay, but he is now literally putting his money where his mouth is. I'm shocked and overwhelmed. Aaron feels like Dr. Wilson felt to me a couple years earlier: one more lifeline sent down from heaven. I'm saved.

19

Chapter 19: A New Low

I contemplate suicide only one more time after coming out to my family and friends.

For the six weeks after Aaron and I talk about investing in a business, I bust my tail looking for an investment opportunity for me to manage. It isn't easy. The one thing in the back of my mind as I research this is the fact that it needs to be a job I can physically perform. Sitting at a desk for thirty minutes hurts. Walking for ten minutes hurts. Grabbing the sugar from the top shelf hurts. With all of my football injuries and surgeries, there are a limited number of things I can do in my management role; whatever it is has to be within my now incredibly limited physical capabilities.

At one point I zero in on a storage facility right near Aaron's hometown of Chico. It isn't glamorous, but it is a smart financial investment that will deliver a return to Aaron. While I'm digging into that I keep the options open, even taking a look at a local Redding bar up for sale. There's a car dealership in the mix too. That's when a real estate agent my family knows tells me about a hotel in Tahoe that's up for sale. It's pretty scuzzy when I go and visit, and some of the hotel guests are renting on a monthly basis. It's that kind of hotel. Aaron hasn't given me much of a guideline for what he's looking for, but I know some of his other investments are in the one- to two-million-dollar range. For only about $700,000, we can buy a classic 1950s hotel with Lake Tahoe private-beach access that has amazing potential. Again, it isn't glamorous but I'm not looking for glamorous. And neither is Aaron. We both simply want an investment that will bring in a solid income with low risk.

The last thing I want to do is lose Aaron money. I know of another guy who I feel is taking advantage of Aaron's kindness and generosity. Aaron complains to me about it from time to time, how his investment in his buddy's business is hemorrhaging money. When you're a guy like Aaron, there are people all around you trying to get a piece of the pie. I don't want a piece of Aaron's pie. I want to grow the size of his pie and feed myself at the same time. I'm okay with accepting some of his help, as long as it means a good return for him. I want to be an investment, not a charity case.

He and I are texting regularly throughout the process, and when I talk to him over the phone right after Christmas he's excited about the project in Tahoe. We decide to hire a contractor to do a soup-to-nuts inspection of the place. We want to know every penny it will take to keep the place running without a complete teardown. No surprises.

When Aaron and I get off the phone that day, I'm as happy as I have been in a long, long time. Coming out to my friends and family has given me hope for the future like I've never experienced in my life. But the weight of my poor financial decisions lingers heavily. Living with my parents in my childhood bedroom is humbling, to put it mildly. Now, for the first time since playing in the NFL, I have something exciting on the horizon, and I will be going into business with a guy I deeply respect, a guy I have called my friend for a decade. It's the perfect arrangement, and we will both come out better for it.

On that call we also talked about a couple of gossip sites on the Internet that have started a rumor about Aaron breaking up with his "boyfriend." That boyfriend is, allegedly, Kevin. The sites pull up photos of the two of them having a good time, traveling together, and doing other things that neither of them ever hid. Kevin has taken to Twitter to share some unkind and esoteric blind items that these sites take as proof that the two were romantically involved. On that phone call I told Aaron to ignore all of the bullshit, and that it would eventually blow over.

Over the holidays I get a contractor lined up and coordinate with the real estate agent to get an inspection done. The real estate agent who connected me to the opportunity is thinking through how exactly to play the acquisition and get the best possible price for Aaron. I text Aaron a few times between Christmas and New Year's for some direction, but I don't hear back from him. It generally isn't unusual for Aaron to not respond to a text. In addition to his schedule, he is prepping to return to the field for the first time since his injury against the Bears. His opponent in that week seventeen end-of-season matchup? The Bears.

That New Year's Eve, Aaron gets on an ESPN Radio show and responds to the gay speculation.

"I'm not gay," he says. "I really, really like women. That's all I can say about that."

Our phone call after Christmas ends up being the last time Aaron ever speaks to me. With no warning, he suddenly cuts off all communication. In the weeks following the holidays, I text him and call him a bunch of times. After that doesn't get a response, I e-mail him a couple times. We had been communicating regularly, and he was going to finance a million-dollar project that I was going to manage. Now nothing. Zero. Radio silence.

I go from thinking my future had, for the first time in my life, some possible light at the end of the tunnel, to feeling lower than I've ever felt in my life. The highest highs produce the lowest lows, and this is the only time since getting sober that I ever again consider suicide. I feel alone and hopeless, having lost my friend and my financial future all at the same time. I never write a suicide note, but the desire to end my life creeps back into my mind. It doesn't linger for years like it had before my coming out. With the coming out of NFL prospect Michael Sam just a few weeks later, and more developments with my disability case (more on this later), my perspective on life continues to improve. But that January is tough. Really tough.

I'll probably never know the full reason Aaron cut off our friendship. Nobody knows better than I that we are all dealing with things under the surface that we think no one else will understand. Some might read this and think Aaron cut off communication with his gay friend when rumors about him being gay came up. This could be the case, but I don't know for sure. Aaron couldn't have been more warm and welcoming when I came out to him. Hell, he was talking about making a big investment in me, knowing full well that I'm gay. He flew me to Green Bay to spend a weekend together. Even after the rumors came out, we still talked, albeit only that once.

As I speak with other mutual friends about Aaron ending our friendship, I learn he has done the same thing to other people. Suddenly Aaron cuts off all communication with them, and they are out of his life overnight. Eventually he even cuts his brothers and parents out of his life. At one point his dad seems to point to "fame" being the cause of it. Except, what NFL quarterback puts his Lombardi Trophy next to the garbage cans in his garage? I don't buy the "he's too famous now" argument. That makes no sense to me. He has clearly made some life choices that I'll probably never know or understand. Aaron has always been an incredibly private person.

I just miss my friend. He was unique in my life. Our football lives intersected through high school, college, and the NFL. And I got to spend two great years with him at Cal. He always made me feel so good about myself, and he always made me feel welcome in his life, always made me smile. I like to think I did the same for him. At one point I definitely get angry with him. Very angry. But as time goes on, that anger turns into hurt. I really loved him (and no, not in THAT way at all).

While I was playing football at Cal and in the NFL, my mom turned my bedroom into a fucking Ryan O'Callaghan shrine. She had gotten the nameplate from my college locker and put it right there on the door, so even before you got into the room you wanted to puke. Inside that room I am Jesus Christ, St. Paul, and Mary mother of God all rolled into one. Even when I was playing I didn't have much use for reminders of my football career around the house, so my mom collected as many of the items that I likely would have just thrown in a box in the garage too. There are trophies I won in high school, game balls I got at Cal, photos, news clippings, you name it.

Living again in my old bedroom, this doesn't sit well with me. Who wants to sleep in a shrine to himself? Not me. Before, I didn't mind my mom saving all that stuff and putting it in my room, even if it was there as a display. But now I am so over football and I don't want to be reminded of it. Here I am, moving into a room where reminders of football literally surround me. My parents know I'm somewhat modest about my accomplishments, and I totally understand they are just proud parents. Still, it doesn't take long for me to clear all that shit out of the room and, yes, put it in boxes in the garage.

I really don't do a whole lot of anything in Redding. Virtually all of my close high school friends have left the area and aren't coming back. Some of the people who have stuck around are either strung out or I just don't feel much of a connection with them. I don't have a job, and frankly, with all of my injuries and chronic pain, I don't know of a job I am fit to do. Standing on my feet for six hours bartending every night isn't possible. Sitting at a desk plugging away at a computer for hours on end is like slowly twisting a steak knife into my shoulder. Instead, a lot of my days are spent in front of the TV watching the clock tick by.

Fuck, my life is boring.

My mom gives me a few things to take care of around the house. I'm thankful for her giving me something to do. After having distanced myself from them for a couple years, there is now a lot of time we have to catch up on, feelings we have to overcome, and fences we have to mend. I still harbor some resentment toward my father over things that went on when I was a kid, and how I often saw him treat my mom. Coming back into their home and spending time with them, we get to talk about some of these things, and I get to see a different side of each of them. I see a better side of them from a wider perspective. This also gives me the chance to reconnect with my sister. We have been mostly disconnected for years, and I have no memory of meeting my nieces and nephew.

Other than getting reacquainted with my family, I am simply not motivated to get off the couch. One thing that does motivate me is the pain. With the painkillers out of my life, I am becoming even more aware of the toll that all of those hits have taken on my body. My left shoulder alone wakes me up every night. Every single night. When I get into my truck I have to pull my left leg into the cab with my hand, because my groin injury has left me unable to lift the leg on its own. My back hurts, my legs hurt . . . fuck it, my entire body from fingers to toes hurts all the time.

One of the things that does start helping again is weed. Since I'm no longer in the NFL, the league isn't testing me for street drugs anymore. I can smoke weed again. I'm a bored former professional athlete whose body hurts all the time everywhere. I know I can never touch the painkillers again. But I've never felt that smoking pot was a problem for me. It really, genuinely helps. I've had some people get on me about drinking alcohol and smoking weed, because of my past addiction. They tell me that if I'm to be truly sober, I have to be *completely* sober. For me, that's bullshit. I appreciate the concern and all, but I don't have a drinking problem and I'm not a pothead. Given my family history and my history with substances, I'm cautious with it.

When I officially retired in 2012, I filed for what the NFL calls "Line of Duty Disability." It's designed to compensate players whose lives have been upended by "substantial disablement arising out of NFL football activities." Of course, they don't make it easy to win a case. If nothing else, I have to get off the couch just to go to the doctor a bunch of times so the NFL can quadruple-check that all of the injuries I amassed in football, and all of the times I ended up on injured reserve, were real and have actually impaired my ability to earn a living. In the end I win that case, which pays a grand total of three thousand dollars a month for three years. Even in Redding, that isn't enough to cover all of my living costs.

This is just the precursor to the bigger fight that awaits me for the NFL's "Total and Permanent Disability." That means the damage my body has suffered in the NFL is so severe that it prevents me from being gainfully employed for the rest of my life. This isn't just going to be a win-and-get-out case, it is going to affect my lifestyle until I die. If I win, I will be prevented from making any kind of a living outside of the settlement. My body is so fucked up from football, I simply don't see any other way out.

My legal fight with the NFL over "Total and Permanent Disability" turns into what seems like a full-time job for about two years. When the NFL is staring down writing a lifetime of checks to one of its former players, they don't go quietly. When I file for the disability, a panel of people at the NFL takes a look at my injuries and my case and quickly denies me benefits.

They claim that somehow football isn't responsible for all of my physical impairments. This is absolutely the worst part of the NFL. The people in the league do everything they can to deny responsibility for the meat grinder the league has created, which chews up the bodies of athletes and spits them out. The notion that my time playing football—and in particular the NFL—is not responsible for my physical injuries is a joke. A mean-spirited joke.

After they deny my case, I have to go to court to prove my disability. The judge assigned to the case puts me through an inquisition. Out of the hundreds of pages of documents and evidence he reviews, he finds the one instance in the past three years of a duck-hunting trip I told my doc about. He grills me about it to see if it shows that I am somehow able to perform manual labor because I could sit in a duck blind for a half hour and aim a gun. I actually appreciate how seriously he takes my case. He isn't going to rubber-stamp the NFL or me. That man takes his job seriously, which is all I ever asked the NFL to do as it was reviewing my case.

In many ways, being a gay man in football has never had this terrible effect on me that so many would expect. There just wasn't an emotional toll imposed on a closeted gay guy in football. I brought *my own* closeted emotional roller coaster to the NFL. Nobody with the Patriots or Chiefs was making antigay comments in the locker room. Hell, at times the atmosphere was downright gay with all the horseplay and towel-snapping.

What doesn't get talked about enough is this physical pounding football players take, and the way it can leave our bodies disabled. The head trauma is certainly making headlines and getting Golden Globe nominations now. But that's just a small part of it. I was essentially slamming myself full speed into a wall every other day for over a dozen years, only to turn around and have the NFL claim my physical ailments have nothing to do with the sport.

Fucking assholes.

Ultimately, the judge rules what was obvious from the start: football, and in particular the NFL, has been the cause of my disability. He sets the date at which I became disabled to 2011, the last time I participated on an NFL field and suffered yet another surgery-requiring shoulder injury. The judgment validates my filing with the NFL, but it also makes me resent the league's front office that much more for their original bullshit ruling that football hadn't sent me to surgery seven times. And counting.

Chapter 20: Coming Out, Interrupted

I'll end up writing off these years from when I'm thirty to when I'm thirty-three, because my life is so dead. Coming out is not some cure-all that immediately washes away years of hiding and guilt and self-hatred. You don't just come out, suddenly find love, and live happily ever after. Learning to live with your true self after lying to everyone around you for so many years takes a lot of work, and a lot of practice.

As a gay man, that practice is hard to find in Redding. Being a conservative area over three hours from a major city, most of the gay people who find themselves in Redding find their way out as fast as they can. The town does have one gay bar, Club 501. But like most smaller-town gay bars, you feel like you know everybody in there after a couple visits. As I start exploring the gay world, I do what a lot of guys do now: I download apps, like Grindr and Tinder. It isn't uncommon to have the tenth-closest guy to me sixty miles away in Chico.

I've still never had sex with another guy. I have never kissed another guy, held another guy's hand. The concept of dating is completely foreign to me. I have never truly dated anyone, man or woman. It's like being a twelve-year-old trapped in a thirty-year-old body, just trying to figure out how to navigate this world of sex and romance that, for the first time, I actually want to be part of.

As I become more comfortable with the fact that I'm gay, and as my life is taking new shape, the desire to get over that hump grows quickly. My thought is that I just need to get the first hookup out of the way, and that experience will somehow give me guidance. While I'm anxious for the first one, I know he has to physically fit my bill. Even without having messed around with other guys, I know what I like. Older—forties or fifties—just doesn't do it for me. Though I'm a bigger guy, I don't find other big guys particularly attractive.

The moment I connect with another football player on Tinder, I'm flipping out. He's on the football team at a community college in Northern California, totally closeted. It's the perfect scenario, like a fantasy come true: somebody whose life I can connect with, and somebody who completely understands where I have been. We are only a few messages in when I tell the guy who I am. Of course, he figures I'm really some random dude in Redding posing as an NFL player to get some shirtless pictures. Eventually I share enough photos of myself that he realizes, *Oh shit, this actually* is *a former NFL player.*

When I get in my truck and head his way a couple days later, there is no pretense about love or romance. He isn't looking for a relationship, and neither am I. I definitely have a few butterflies swirling around my stomach, but mostly I'm excited for what the next twenty-four hours hold. A lot of gay people have to deal with religious guilt, but I've never had that feeling. There isn't a care in the world what some "god" might think about what I'm about to do. My whole issue with being gay has been about other people rejecting me. I couldn't ever have sex with another guy because I couldn't give anyone any reason to believe I'm gay. Now that I see the love and acceptance around me, I'm ready to dive in.

Last night I went online and rented a room at a hotel near

his campus. After I check in and see the room, I give him a call and tell him to come over. I wait for him in the parking lot, my toes tapping the pavement with excitement. When he pulls up in his car and gets out of the driver's seat, the toe-tapping stops and I take an audible gulp. He is *beautiful*. About six feet tall, clearly in great shape—a football player, but not one of the big guys on the line.

I get to have sex with him??!!

We share a couple of "heys" and head to the room, exchanging small talk as we walk down the hall. He's the local guy still in the closet, so we go in the side door and up the stairs to the room so nobody sees us walking through the lobby together. I have a room with a king-size bed, figuring nothing smaller would fit two football players. When we get in the room we both sit on the bed and chat a bit about football. I've closed the shades so there isn't any paranoia on his part, and I've left on only one light so it isn't too bright. We spend a couple hours together that afternoon.

After he leaves and I'm standing in the shower, the hot water pouring over me and steaming up the bathroom, I start to chuckle. This whole episode has been so easy, so comfortable. Even that afternoon, my first time naked and alone with another guy, it all felt so much more normal to me than any time I've been with a woman. I've known I'm gay for my entire adult life, but it's only now that I realize how I knew: my attraction to men has always just felt normal to me. It may seem so abnormal to other people, particularly most guys in football, but to me it is so comfortable, so easy, so real. I don't have to fake excitement or interest. Everything just works.

What the hell was the big deal?

He and I will never communicate again. Neither of us ever even try.

* * *

The first guy I start dating regularly—where the word "boyfriend" enters my mind, even if we don't say it—lives in Eureka, a California coastal town about two hours away. We have, it seems, both swiped the same direction on Tinder. I'm a little surprised when I get the match. In just a couple years of being out, I have quickly learned that most gay guys seem to like abs and 0 percent body fat. No, I'm not pointing fingers. I've found myself gravitating toward those very same guys. While I have come way down from my Cal playing weight of 370, I don't even have a two-pack. Yet what I quickly learn from Brandon is that big men like me do have a gay fan base, including some guys like him who have the six-pack.

Brandon is a ball of energy and super fun to be around. He's just what I need in my first foray into the gay dating world. He's always positive, which really helps me. I often have trouble being especially positive as I'm still dealing with so many transitions in my life, so being around that attitude is the best possible medicine for me.

Shortly after we start dating, I get word that I've been selected to the Shasta County Sports Hall of Fame. At the induction ceremony there will be a bunch of local sports dignitaries, friends and family, a dinner, and some speeches. The local media will also be there, and that gets me thinking. NFL prospect Michael Sam came out publicly just a few months ago. Shortly afterward, Scott Pioli called me for advice. He was with the Atlanta Falcons by then, and he wanted my take on whether Sam could fit into an NFL locker room. If anyone in the NFL wanted to make a statement by selecting Sam for their team, it was Scott. That's just the kind of guy he is, always trying to help minorities get a foothold in the league. I told Scott that I just wasn't sure, but that all of the guys in the league I'd come out to had been really supportive. And if Sam had a guy like Scott he could lean on in the organization, it could work. Sam ended up being drafted by the Rams, and his experience really gets me wondering if adding my story to the conversation about gay athletes could help.

By the time the awards banquet rolls around, I've settled on a plan. Almost every honoree brings a date to these things, and they always thank that date for their support. Since I'm dating Brandon, I'll bring him along, mention him in my speech, and let the media there run wild with it.

My dad doesn't like my plan very much at all. The night before the event, he pulls me aside and asks me if I'm sure this is what I want to do. His questions are about me and my well-being, but it really seems like he just doesn't want to deal with me being gay and having it all over the media. I'm still living with my parents, and Dad obviously knows he has a gay son living in his house, but in some ways I think it still isn't real for him. I'm the same guy I always was, I never date, and I never talk about being gay. He shares his concerns with me, but I'm all-in on the plan.

The next day, a couple hours before the ceremony, everybody meets at my parents' house. My sister, my brother-in-law, a couple friends, and Brandon. It's hard not to like Brandon the moment you meet him, but I'm afraid of how my dad will react shaking hands with a guy he knows I'm dating, a guy I've kissed. Thankfully, Brandon is his ever-bubbly, friendly self, and he melts my dad's armor as soon as he walks in the house. Meeting Brandon that night finally makes having a gay son very real for my dad. Sharing a laugh with Brandon certainly doesn't hurt.

The ceremony is being held at the Big League Dreams facility in Redding, which has a bunch of sporting venues like baseball diamonds and basketball courts. They've dressed up one of the basketball courts with some tables and a stage for the dinner and presentation. I'm excited to meet soccer player Megan Rapinoe, another local athlete in my induction class. She came out a couple years ago and represents the United States in the World Cup. She's badass. But when I get there I find out she has sent in a video instead of showing up herself. I'm bummed, but the truth is, if I had still been in the NFL I probably wouldn't have been able to make it either.

Dinner is a lot of chitchatting with my family and friends and catching up with a couple people I haven't seen in a while. I introduce "my boyfriend Brandon" to as many people as I can that night. Some people know I'm gay, and some don't, but I figure introducing someone to a guy I'm dating is the most low-key way to let people know.

Of course, the entire time I'm thinking about my speech and the public reaction. Telling a couple locals is one thing; telling the world is another. When it comes time for me to accept the award, I rise from my seat to polite applause. I had written out some remarks on a piece of paper so I won't screw up what I want to say. I pull that out of my coat pocket, get behind the podium, and start thanking the usual suspects. Then I let it out.

"I also want to thank my boyfriend Brandon, who came all the way from Eureka to be here with me tonight."

I don't know what I was expecting, but whatever it was, it doesn't happen. People sit there quietly, just listening to what I have to say. It reminds me of Scott's reaction, how he couldn't even understand that what I was telling him was somehow news.

After my speech, people come up and congratulate me, but not a word about Brandon.

The next day in the newspapers? Crickets. Nobody writes about it, nobody reports on it. No one seems to give a shit that this former NFL player just told the world that he's gay. I'm actually pretty disappointed.

Truth is, I quickly realize they have all done me a huge favor. I am not ready to come out publicly. I'm still struggling with it a bit, finding my gay way in the world, despite the veneer I try to put on. At this point, I'm where most sixteen-year-olds are in their sexual development. I'm figuring out how to date, how to talk to people I'm interested in, how to find them. I want to help other people, be a resource for other gay guys struggling with who they are. But you can't really give advice to other people if you haven't fully lived. I need to live life as a gay man. I need to learn. I need to focus a lot more on understanding myself and expanding my horizons, and a lot less on worrying about heaping a bunch of responsibility on my shoulders.

A couple days later, my dad says the most shocking three words I have ever heard come out of his mouth: "Brandon seemed nice."

Those three little words tell me that he is truly coming around, that his full acceptance of his gay son is on the horizon. He's trying to understand me better, trying to become closer to me. Living together back in high school, and even now as I'm trying to recover from the NFL, has created wedges in our relationship. This day is a turning point for us.

Not long after that dinner, Brandon and I break up. Even with all of his positive energy, I feel myself wanting to see what else is out there. We aren't the perfect match, and I know there is more I can be feeling when I'm with another guy than how I feel with him. But his impact on my family and me has huge positive repercussions. My dad doesn't seem to shudder anymore at the idea that he has a gay son. And while I am blessed that no media have picked up the story of me being gay, having Brandon there that night and seeing the nonreaction of so many people makes me even more determined to get my life right and, when I have my ducks in a row, use my story to truly help other people.

Chapter 21: The Plunge

It's May 2017 and I've decided I am finally, truly ready. I have been embroiled in a years-long legal battle with the NFL over my disability claims, and that has turned out okay. In the deal, I get paid a decent amount every year, but I can't make a living of any kind outside of that. The annual disability payment should be double what it is, but still, it's enough to live on.

With that more or less behind me, I can move on to the next big thing: helping as many other people as I can.

Ever since Michael Sam came out, I have been thinking about sharing my story publicly. I've been disappointed with the way his story ended. Falling down the draft board (I certainly know how that feels), failing to make the final roster of an NFL team, fizzling out in the Canadian Football League. Three years later, Sam's was still the last story about a gay NFL player to be told. Everybody has seemed to keep quiet after that. And this sucks. I had made it in the NFL. I had played in the Super Bowl. I had helped the Patriots to an undefeated regular season. And I had been to hell and back.

I remember how much seeing Ellen DeGeneres come out helped me when I was a teenager. Being in Redding, surrounded by antigay chatter, seeing her speak so confidently about who she was—it certainly helped me twenty years ago. I'm of course not the household name she is. I don't have my own TV show.

Hell, most people in New England and Kansas City have forgotten I ever existed. But I know that sharing my story can help some young football player in Tennessee or Idaho, or even Redding. And if I can make one kid feel better about himself or herself, feel like he or she isn't alone and has someone to talk to, then I owe it to that kid to break my public silence.

For the last couple of years I've been following a website called Outsports.com. They write a lot about gay athletes, and in particular they tell the coming-out stories of a lot of athletes and coaches across sports. One of their writers, Cyd Zeigler, has grabbed my interest. I really like how he writes his stories, and I have often connected to what he's saying. When I contact him on Facebook, I'm shocked by his response. *Yeah, I know who you are*, he writes. *I'm a lifelong Patriots fan. So I was trying to figure out "Is this really Ryan O'Callaghan?"*

Over the next couple of weeks we chat on the phone for hours and hours. If I'm going to tell my story, I don't want to hide a thing. I open up to him about my suicide plans, my fears about being gay, about the drugs . . . all of it. I had shared bits and pieces of my struggle with a bunch of friends and family, but suddenly I'm sharing my whole story, almost every little detail, with some writer I met on Facebook. I'm telling him things I have never told anybody. It feels good.

The rollout of my story is going to feature the video of a sit-down interview, so I plan a weekend trip to Los Angeles in early June. It's Pride weekend down there, when the whole city will be celebrating the gay community. I've never been to a Pride celebration before, and my introduction is the Pride Night at the Los Angeles Dodgers game that Friday night. Cyd has gotten us passes to the owners' suite, where I get to meet gay former Major League Baseball player Billy Bean and singer Lance Bass, along with a bunch of other people.

I'm a nervous wreck. I'm downing cheap margaritas almost as fast as the bartender can make them. I feel it. Being around all of the rainbow flags and all of the gay people is completely overwhelming. Of course, no one has any fucking clue who I am. When you plan to break a story like a former NFL player coming out, there's a lot of playing it close to the vest that goes into it. You don't want anyone tweeting out the news or anything else until you're ready for the story to break. That night I'm just Cyd's friend Ryan who used to play football. And it freaks me the fuck out.

The next day we record the video interview in the baking sun at UCLA. I have always been so self-conscious of my propensity to sweat, and now I feel like I'm a soaking-wet mess. I finish that interview fast enough and get out of the hot LA sun. That night Cyd drags me to a bar in West Hollywood called The Chapel. I felt uncomfortable at the Dodgers' Pride Night, but at the bar in WeHo on the Saturday night of Los Angeles Pride, I feel downright out of place. Between the pounding dance music, the waving rainbow flags, the half-naked men, and the twentysomethings swinging their carefree hands in the air, it's like nothing I have ever seen. I'm gay, no question about that. And I like hanging around gay guys. What is going on at that gay bar, the epicenter of gay life in LA, however, is all just beyond anything I have ever seen, and it's quickly too much for me. I leave after less than an hour.

Flying out of LA the next day, having processed everything I saw, I find myself actually wanting more. Being gay in Redding just isn't what I have in mind for my life right now. Sure, I hadn't even planned to still be alive at age thirty-four. But what I see in the gay community in LA isn't just existence, it's joy. Fun. Maybe the dancing boys at The Chapel aren't quite my thing yet, but I realize on this trip that I am keeping myself completely sheltered from the gay community and really limiting my ability to fully express myself.

In the coming days I get more and more excited about my story running, not just because it represents an opportunity to help other people, but it might also provide a chance to connect with other gay guys in and out of sports—the kinds of connections that are simply impossible to make in Shasta County.

In the days before the story runs, I barely sleep a wink. All of the emotions of the last twenty years are spinning in my head all night long. Plus, the story is out of my hands. Two days before the release date Cyd tells me I'm not going to be able to see the story before it appears, and I just have to trust him.

Fuck that!

I've reconnected with Scott Pioli ahead of the story, and having him along for the ride with me for its release is super important to me. He gave me confidence and friendship when I needed it most as I was coming out to people in my life. Now that I'm coming out publicly, he's there on the phone with me just about every day, offering me encouragement and telling me it will all work out. It's also nice to reconnect with Dr. Wilson. I might not be alive today if it weren't for her and Dave Price. She tells me she's really happy to hear from me, and that I've obviously landed on my feet.

I ask to have my e-mail included at the bottom of the story so that anyone who feels like he or she needs help can reach out to me. In 2014, I had been completely unequipped to be of any help. In 2017, I have now lived life as a gay man for five years. I have been down a lot of roads and learned a lot about myself and the community. I'm ready to help.

I don't sleep much that night, par for the course. Every person I have come out to up to this point has reacted positively to my news. Still, when you're told almost all your life that being gay is a bad thing you have to hide from everyone in your world, and especially the sports world, doubt settles in. My mind jumps around like a jackrabbit that night. A little bit of weed calms me down a bit, and I get a few Z's.

When I finally get out of bed the next morning, it feels like I am watching an explosion in slow motion. My phone has already buzzed a couple times on the nightstand. By the time I actually swing my legs off the side of the bed, the buzzing literally will not stop. I look at my phone. Notifications for a few text messages, a few dozen Facebook friend requests, and almost a hundred e-mails stare back.

One of the first phone calls I get that morning is from Mike Vrabel. All those years later he still has my number in his phone. He just wants to reach out and tell me that he's proud of me and totally supports me. Dustin calls too, along with a bunch of other former teammates from Cal and the NFL. Most of these guys are finding out I'm gay for the very first time. They aren't just supporting me in my public coming out, they are supporting me as a gay man.

I quickly realize I'm not quite ready for the massive response to my story. In the first few hours I receive literally thousands of e-mails from people all around the world. Almost all of them are total strangers. I sit down and go through as many e-mails as I can handle, but I can't come close to keeping up. Reading every word, it blows me away that people would sit down and spend time writing paragraphs, spilling their life story to a total stranger. There are also phone calls and messages from *Sports Illustrated*, ESPN, *USA Today*, writers, movie producers, book publishers, all suddenly interested in me and my story. It's so overwhelming that by noon I'm feeling like I might have an anxiety attack.

Thank god I don't have any Vicodin in the house.

"Shut off your phone, make yourself a margarita, and go sit in the pool," Cyd says over the phone. "Everybody can wait an hour while you take some time for yourself."

It's great advice, and I do just that. Though it doesn't last long. Sitting there in the pool watching Taylor and Rodger run around the backyard, my mind travels to small-town America, where there's a kid a lot like me stumbling across my story and for the first time thinking, *I'm not the only one.* The idea of missing that kid's e-mail cuts my break short, the curiosity and nervous excitement spinning around in my head and getting the best of me. I'm quickly back out of the pool, drying myself off, and sitting back down to read more e-mails.

As the day wears on, many of the e-mails aren't quick hellos—some of these people are writing their own feature-length life-story articles and sending it to me. Some of them say they've never told a soul they're gay. Others haven't been able to reconcile it with themselves, but they know beyond a doubt they're "different." I find myself needing to respond to as many as I possibly can.

By nightfall I have already received five thousand e-mails from across the globe. Two of those e-mails in particular make me know that the whole process of publicly coming out is very worthwhile.

One is a former NFL star who has a secret just like mine. When I first see his name pop up, I don't think much of it. Again, I'm just not an NFL fan. If you aren't Joe Montana, and you weren't lining up opposite me on a Sunday, chances are I don't know your name. When I look up his name on Google, I certainly recognize him after that. He tells me he has been struggling to figure out how to come out in his own life, and he has a complication I just don't have: kids.

He reiterates a concern I've heard from a bunch of guys: that it just feels awkward to sit down with your family and friends and blurt out, "I'm gay" or "I'm bi." I can certainly relate to that. Instead, he's looking to date another guy, as introducing family and friends to a boyfriend will just make the whole conversation a lot more organic. I get it completely. Dad meeting Brandon helped shift the dynamic of our relationship, made me being different tangible for him. I'm not quite sure if this former NFL player is looking to date me in particular, but he starts sending some vibes. I don't bite, as it's just not in the cards. Even so, I remain a pair of ears to listen and empathize like very few other people could.

Of all the people who message me, maybe the most memorable is a straight guy from a town a lot like Redding, a guy a lot like my dad. His son had come out to him awhile back, and the guy disowned his son for it. It's everything I had always feared would be my parents' reaction to me coming out to them. The guy pours his heart out to me, telling me that reading my story has made him rethink how he's treated his gay son. He says he now realizes that far worse than having a gay son would be getting a phone call that his son has taken his own life because he didn't have support. Then he tells me that my story has driven him to reach out to his son to make amends. I shed some tears over that one.

Every time somebody of note comes out, I see messages on social media asking, *Who cares?* That mentality comes from people who really don't want anyone talking about gay shit because it makes them uncomfortable. They themselves care so little that they take time out of their day to ask who cares. I'm sure Sigmund Freud would have had a thing or two to say about that. What I find on that very first day my story runs, and that I will continue to learn for months to come, is that *lots* of people care. So many more than I ever could have imagined.

These two e-mails—knowing that sharing my story helps people I've never met—makes everything worth it.

But I never hear from Aaron.

Two months later I'm heading up Park Avenue in New York City. Destination: NFL headquarters. The league is hosting an event launching their new NFL Pride initiative, an employee resource group for LGBTQ people in the NFL. They ask me, along with former NBA player Jason Collins and MLB executive Billy Bean, to be part of a panel discussion addressing LGBTQ inclusion in pro sports. The league is trying to take concrete steps, both internally and externally, to build a more inclusive environment in and around the NFL. There's going to be a prepanel reception with wine and food, and most of the people in the front office are expected to attend. Why? Because Commissioner Roger Goodell is on the guest list, and he RSVP'd "yes." When the commish shows up to an event like that in your own office, you better be there. Plus, it's personal for him—Goodell's brother is gay.

Scott Pioli even flies in for the event. It's specifically for league front-office employees, but he comes all the way from Atlanta, in the middle of the Falcons' training camp, to be there to support me at this NFL Pride event. When I tell you that Scott is the real, genuine guy who did nothing but support me my entire career, long after I could ever do a thing for him, that is exactly the guy he is. He probably couldn't care less whether Goodell is there or not. I'm going to be there, and he figures having a familiar face in the room will be a help. It is.

I'm excited to meet Goodell—not to talk to him about my struggles as a gay athlete, but about the league's drug policy, the ban of pot, and most importantly, the bullshit system I had to go through to show that football had left me with a disability. There aren't many times you get the chance to talk to the NFL commissioner, and I am going to go right into his house and tell him how unhappy I am with it all, how patently unfair it is.

When I was playing, if you were being called into the NFL front office, it wasn't to sip chardonnay with the commish. It's the last place a player wants to go. But walking through the doors of the league is like strolling into a local Bank of America branch for me. Sure, it's neat to get the invitation, and it's cool to walk the halls of the league front office—it really is beautiful. I just don't get any shivers walking past Lombardi Trophies or Super Bowl rings.

What I do enjoy is meeting Billy Bean and Jason Collins. I had actually met Billy at that Dodgers Pride Night a couple weeks before my story hit, but I just couldn't talk about anything at the time so he had no idea I played in the NFL. Now that I'm free to share who I am, it's cool just shooting the shit with them. There aren't many guys who have played pro sports and come out publicly, though it's not like we actually talked about any of that. Being in the presence of these gay pro athletes I had read about is like being welcomed into a fraternity I once thought couldn't possibly exist.

Just as our panel discussion starts, Goodell walks in. I'm a little bummed because I figure he'll stay a few minutes, listen to several comments so he can say he was there, and be on his way. He is the commissioner of the biggest pro sports league in North America. He has other shit to do, and I probably won't get the chance to corner him on my issues.

Instead, he stays for the entire discussion. I glance over at him a few times as Jason, Billy, and I speak, and he isn't just sitting in the back tapping away at his phone—he's standing at the front of the room listening intently. We talk on the panel for maybe forty minutes, and when it's over Goodell comes right up to me and shakes my hand.

"That was great, Ryan. Thanks for coming all this way."

What the fuck was I so afraid of?

"What can I do as the commissioner to help other closeted gay players in the league?"

I'm the perfect person for his question. Unfortunately, I don't have the perfect answer. Part of me is still spinning the issue of disability in my head, wanting so much to unload on him about their ridiculous system. But his questions are genuine and disarming, and I want to give him whatever insight I can.

"Your visible support goes a long way," I say. "Keep talking about the issue and keep having events like this. It helps."

Goodell hangs out with Jason, Billy, and me for a good half hour after the event, introducing us to other league executives. Of all the people I meet at the league office that day, it's Goodell in particular who's the most interested and the most engaged in what we're doing. After all I went through with the league—the addiction, the drug tests, the disability fight—the last thing I ever expected was that when I was finally in a room with the man at the top, I would actually like him. He isn't this maniacal tyrant smoking cigars and dictating people's lives from behind a desk on Park Avenue. He's a real guy. He asks real questions. He listens. He laughs. He has every excuse in the world to bolt out of that room as soon as he can, but he doesn't.

I had entered that room looking to throw some punches. Instead I end up shaking hands. They have no idea that inside of me I'm steaming about so much I have seen in the NFL. I decide right there in the middle of the event, celebrating gay athletes, just isn't the right time to have some of the other tough conversations that need to be had in the league.

As I leave, headed into the sun setting on the streets of

Manhattan, I vow that I will do my best to return to 345 Park Avenue and have a very different conversation with some of the people in that room.

The NFL engages me much more in the next year. They feature me on their New York City Pride float the following June, marking a year since I came out publicly. That's pretty cool. They also fly me down to the 2018 Pro Bowl in Orlando, where they are doing some youth outreach. The other featured guest at the event is Esera Tuaolo, the gay former defensive end who had given the talk at the NFL Rookie Symposium just as I was entering the league.

He and I have an absolute blast together, these two gay giants who spent so many years in the league having hours of laughs over beer and cocktails at Disney's Animal Kingdom. I give him shit about his Rookie Symposium talk making me scared as hell, and he gives it right back to me. Esera is really fun to be around, a very cool, down-to-earth guy. That night I also get to meet Landon Foster, a former punter for the University of Kentucky. Just like with Billy and Jason, it's cool to meet other guys in the "fraternity" who have had so many of the same fears and have walked a similar path as mine.

Other incredible opportunities continue to pop up to talk about the life I now see for gay athletes. When Congressman Joe Kennedy invites me to join him for Boston Pride, it gives me the chance to share my thoughts on the possibility of an openly gay player on the New England Patriots, something I think would today be completely embraced by the team, including the ownership and the coaching staff. Nike makes me part of an event designed to inspire youth in the Portland, Oregon, area to be true to themselves. Countless people reach out via e-mail and social media for help. I still try to answer every single person and share with them whatever insights about life I think can help them in their journey.

Cal really steps up too. Walking the halls of Memorial Stadium and sitting down with members of the football team there is some of the most rewarding advocacy I've gotten to do since coming out. It brings me back "home" to where I spent the most time playing football in my life. It opens my eyes to the current state of athletes in big-time sports. By and large, they just don't care if their teammate is gay. They only care if you're able to pancake that defensive end.

I've even started a foundation to help fund the college education of LGBTQ athletes who find the courage to be their true selves and let the world know who they really are.

After all those years of feeling alone, I appreciate on a daily basis all of the support that surrounds me today. I've come to the conclusion that this support has actually always been there. I just couldn't see it. Whatever issue I needed help with—being gay, the drug addiction, sinking into depression—I had the love and support of my family, the people in football, and even perfect strangers who had no idea what kind of person was wrestling with life under that helmet.

 *Epilogue*

The phone rings at the ungodly morning hour of seven fifteen. Rodger and Taylor stir on the bed, as disappointed as I am with the phone. I ignore it for a moment, then think it might be my boyfriend Strand rolling me out of bed as he heads to class. I finally grab the phone, ready to tell him to have a nice day but stop calling so early. Instead, when I look at the caller ID, I see *Gillette Stadium.* I clear my throat and answer.

"Ryan, this is Robert Kraft from the New England Patriots." My voice is clearly still a bit crackly so he follows that up with, "Oh, it's probably early there. If you want, I can call you back later."

I sit right up and assure him it's a great time to talk. A few days before, the NFL had invited me to be part of an LGBTQ outreach program at the 2017 NFL Kickoff between my two former teams. Mr. Kraft apparently got wind of it and he wanted to personally make a phone call to me. Now that he has me on the phone, he talks about his gay friend, Elton John. One of the things I've found is that since coming out, people want to relate to me by sharing stories about their gay friends. Of course, Mr. Kraft's gay friend is one of the most well-known singers in the world, whom I had seen perform at his anniversary party. Because that's how billionaires roll.

"I'm having a reception before the game, and I'd love for

you to come," Mr. Kraft says of the upcoming Kickoff game. "I can show you the new trophy."

As the defending Super Bowl champions, the Patriots are hosting the first game of the season. In 2007 we had come up just a play short, leaving me with my conference champion "losers' ring." Mr. Kraft loves his Lombardi Trophies, and he has said very publicly that he is most proud of the one for the 2016 season. He and the Patriots aren't too happy with how Goodell and the league handled some badly inflated footballs. It seems even billionaires can have issues with the folks on Park Avenue.

By now it has sunk in: Robert Kraft is personally calling me on my phone and inviting me to join him at a reception in Foxborough. That's not exactly a phone call you get every day. He tells me that he had tried to call when I came out a few months earlier, but he was on a trip in Israel and they had the wrong phone number. He wants the chance to talk with me personally.

I accept.

The day before the NFL Kickoff game I work with the league at an event for LGBTQ kids from across Southeastern Massachusetts. We spend the day at Gillette Stadium meeting former players, team staff, and these kids. They teach me a ton. I never knew what "cisgender" meant. Now I know. But mostly I'm in awe of these kids who seem so comfortable with who they are. Gay kids, queer, transgender. It took me thirty-four years to get where they just naturally seem to arrive by their early teens.

The most heartbreaking moment of the event in Foxborough is watching these gay and transgender youth packing up boxes of food from the reception. My eyes can't stop following them leaving with plastic bags filled with chicken wings and french fries. It isn't because they are the best wings they've ever had, it's because they might not have dinner that night if they don't take some food with them. I learn that day that a black transgender woman's life expectancy is under thirty-five years. It really hits me that not all LGBTQ people get to live the life I live. While I'm complaining about my six-figure-per-year settlement with the NFL, these kids are just trying to find the next meal. It certainly puts life into perspective.

That night I meet Dustin Colquitt in Providence, Rhode Island. He is still punting and preaching for the Chiefs. While we are a thousand miles from Kansas City, spending a few minutes with him feels like a homecoming. He is staying at the team hotel with the Chiefs, and my driver is instructed by the NFL to take me wherever I want. All I want to do is see my old friend, but it's also nice to run into some of the staff from the team who had seen my story and recognize me. They all say really nice things, just like everybody else.

When Dustin is done with his meetings for the night, he meets me in the lobby. He tells me he has taken inspiration from my deer plots in Missouri and has set up some deer cameras near the Chiefs' practice facility. He and several of the guys have taken to watching for deer, and they are doing bow-and-arrow practice there on a regular basis. Even though I have long since sold my cabin and the property, Dustin is still finding ways to get his hands dirty in nature, and he's sharing that with the other guys on the team. In some small way, I feel like I have had an impact on the culture of the Chiefs. That really feels good.

"You seem very happy," Dustin says at the end of our visit. The only Ryan O'Callaghan he had known was a guy sinking into drugs and depression, writing a suicide note at night and building his own crypt. Now I am, for maybe the first time in my life, finding actual happiness.

* * *

When I arrive at Mr. Kraft's reception, I'm not sure what to think of it all. I'm walking in alone, and I haven't been with the team for a decade. Almost immediately I see Matt Light and his wife. I love Matt. Everybody loves Matt. We talk about a couple ventures of his—one a light vodka company and the other some lumber salvaging. Matt is always up to something. He is quick to get one of his vodka drinks in my hand. It's actually pretty good.

Kevin Faulk is there too. He was one of the running backs on the team the whole time I was with the Patriots. He asks me a dozen questions about being gay, but he's mostly interested in hearing about my surviving suicidal thoughts. Turns out someone in his life has been dealing with suicidal thoughts as well, and Kevin just wants some insight into what he should do. It makes me proud to be there to help him navigate it in some small way.

Andre Tippett also makes sure to track me down.

"I'm so proud of you and what you've done," he says. He played for the Patriots well before I got there, but everybody who spends time in and around the organization knows Andre, one of the hardest-hitting Patriots of all time. He tells me about a gay person close to him in his life—almost everybody has at least one—and how much of an influence that person has had on him. When I tell him about this book I'm writing, and my creation a foundation to help other gay athletes, he's all-in.

"Let me know if you need help with any of that, Ryan. I mean that. *Anything.*"

As I survey the room, talking with Matt and Kevin and Dan Koppen and Deion Branch and other guys, it hits me how far I have come, how many lives I have affected both before and after I shared my story. I was an offensive lineman who was with the Patriots for only three seasons. Yet the guys know me, they have read my story. And they aren't at all afraid to come up to me and talk to the gay guy. In fact, it feels like they really want to.

I'm ultimately led to Mr. Kraft himself, whom I haven't seen for almost a decade. He's a shorter man with a big personality, and I have to bend down as he opens up his arms to embrace me.

"What you did took a lot of courage," he says into my ear. "I'm so proud of you."

He then introduces me to a couple other people standing around him. At one point he grabs actor Mark Wahlberg and makes sure to have the two of us shake hands. When you're a billionaire owner of a perennial Super Bowl champion, the rich and famous find their way to you. Mr. Kraft tells Mark all about my story and how proud he is to have me as a Patriot. Then, after a few more minutes of introducing me around, Mr. Kraft leads me to his private office just off the side of the room. His office is, as would be expected, spectacular. Awards and plaques adorn the walls, with dark wood bringing a homey feel to his massive space. His huge desk sits on the far end of the room, near the windows. When you build your own stadium, you get to have the office of your dreams.

As we continue to catch up, Mr. Kraft walks to his wooden desk and opens the top drawer. "Ryan, did you bring a friend with you tonight? I have a couple tickets for you."

Damnit. Why didn't I bring Strand?

"It's just me." I left my boyfriend back in California as this was supposed to be a "work trip." Mr. Kraft tells me he has a block of club-level tickets that he always reserves, and if I ever want to attend another game I should let him know.

"What you have done is so courageous," he tells me again as he hands me the game ticket. "I am so proud that you are forever a Patriot."

Spending a few minutes privately with Mr. Kraft in his office is surreal. It's just him and me, with a couple hundred people outside his office door clamoring for his attention and thousands more pouring into the stadium outside his office window. I never got that treatment when I was on his payroll. I reflect in these moments on the fact that he wants to spend this time with me—billionaires, I've learned, do exactly what they want to do. For Mr. Kraft, who opens up to me about a gay friend, I am the most important person in the world in those few moments. Given where I have been in the previous dozen years, he is equally the most important person in the world for me right then and there.

Sitting in Mr. Kraft's seats for the game reinforces all of this.

Watching the Chiefs pummel the Patriots on that surreal opening night, I have an empty seat on my left. Strand, or some other friend, could have been there. I don't even have any gay friends in New England to call up last-minute. I was entirely closeted the whole time I was there. That empty seat serves as a reminder of all the years I spent alone.

On my right are two men, straight guys, best friends who had driven to the game together from Cape Cod. They recognize me and start asking me questions about the Patriots, and Tom Brady in particular.

"Tom is the world's fastest beer chugger," I tell them. It's true. They eat it up.

As the game wears on, they tell me about their wives, who had left these guys for each other. Yes, their ex-wives are lesbians who fell in love and now live together. We watch the game and talk and share, each of them pouring a bit more of his heart out to me. They tell me all about Provincetown, a pretty gay little town at the tip of Cape Cod.

"That is literally the last place on earth you would have ever found me back then," I say. Now, of course, it sounds like a lot of fun.

The three of us bond that day. Two straight guys and a gay guy having some laughs and beer over all kinds of shit as we watch two NFL teams duke it out. It's a powerful moment for me. It reflects so many of my experiences since coming out. Literally every day I'm blown away by stories of how LGBTQ people have affected the lives of Americans around them. Could be a gay son, a lesbian wife. Everybody seems to have a story. They're stories I wouldn't have believed a decade ago. I didn't *want* to believe them.

Since sharing my story, and seeing how it has helped other people, I've repeatedly wondered what the fuck I was so afraid of. But the most important thing I keep reminding myself about isn't my past but my future.

My life isn't on the line anymore.

The National Suicide Prevention Lifeline
1-800-273-8255

The Lifeline provides 24/7, free, and confidential support
for people in distress.